Presented To:

_____

From:

_____

Date:

_____

AWAKENING

THE ONE

NEW MAN

ROBERT F. WOLFF

EDITING BY DON ENEVOLDSEN

Editing by Don Enevoldsen

DESTINY IMAGE® PUBLISHERS, INC.
P.O. Box 310, Shippensburg, PA 17257-0310

"Speaking to the Purposes of God for This Generation and for the Generations to Come."

This book and all other Destiny Image, Revival Press, MercyPlace, Fresh Bread, Destiny Image Fiction, and Treasure House books are available at Christian bookstores and distributors worldwide.

For a U.S. bookstore nearest you, call 1-800-722-6774.
For more information on foreign distributors, call 717-532-3040.
Reach us on the Internet: www.destinyimage.com.

ISBN 13 TP: 978-0-7684-3854-3
ISBN 13 Ebook: 978-0-7684-8971-2

For Worldwide Distribution, Printed in the U.S.A.

1 2 3 4 5 6 7 8 9 10 11 / 13 12 11

Acknowledgments

My deepest gratitude for the assistance of so many. My family has never failed to stand by me. I dedicate this endeavor to my wonderful wife, Wendy, and our children Luka, Kai, and Lee, and to their love and acceptance. To those who have gone before, both nuclear and extended family—our spiritual fathers and mothers in the faith—thank you for paving the way for myself and countless others to follow.

The seed for this ministry was planted as "Majestic Glory" and was launched with a vision to awaken the Children of God to His calling to walk as *One New Man*.

Jean Cadet first encouraged me to open the door to *Awakening the One New Man*. Coach McCartney added his endorsement and support. Ray Gannon wholeheartedly embraced, guided, and engineered this endeavor, as well as introduced me to several of these authors. From that time until now, so many have said yes. To these and to each of our authors, words cannot adequately express my appreciation.

A special word of gratitude, to Don Enevoldsen. Works like this don't take their shape or have their being without someone who tirelessly brings all the pieces together. That is Don's gift to me, and now to you.

For those who have prayed, written, warred, critiqued, and encouraged, I am humbled to stand alongside you. The Lord knows this is your book as well as mine, and it all belongs to Him.

Bless your hearts,
Bob

Endorsements

Awakening the One New Man is a serious subject that has long needed to be addressed. In reading this inspiring collection of essays, I would urge everybody in Christ to be engaged in this profound vision. I certainly would commit Mount Carmel Ministries International in South Africa to this vision with the urgency, love, and compassion that it deserves.

Desmond Peterson,
Mount Carmel Ministries International,
Johannesburg

Yes, there is an Awakening taking place. These gifted authors bring a message that invites all believers in the God of Israel to stand as one. This is the time and the season of the Lord's calling for Jew and Gentile to embrace our identity in the Jewish Messiah and Redeemer of the nations, Yeshua (Jesus) of Nazareth.

Joel Chernoff
MJAA General Secretary/CEO

I encourage you to absorb this wealth of wisdom from a stunning collection of authors, who are preparing us to be the One New Man, the Bride of our Coming King.

Mike Bickle,
International House of Prayer,
Kansas City

The history of hostility between Jews and Gentiles has been a hall of shame. Our Savior paid the ultimate price to demolish this wall of hostility and create one new man out of the two. This book challenges us to keep this wall from rising again and offers us God's roadmap to peace.

Pastor Wayne Hilsden
King of Kings Community
Jerusalem

Contents

Foreword

Years ago, I preached a sermon about the diversity and inclusiveness of the local Church. The Church, I said, should reflect the diversity of its society, and it should welcome people to hear and experience the Gospel regardless of where they come from. I mentioned religious background as one example. Assemblies of God, Baptist, Catholic, Jewish, Muslim, unbeliever—the Church should welcome them all, for Jesus Christ (Yeshua haMashiach) loves them all.

After the service, my son ran up to me, excited by an idea he had thought up during my sermon. He was seven or eight years old at the time. He took notes on all my sermons.

"Dad, I got it! I got it!" he said. "What this church is supposed to be. We'll call the balcony the KG balcony." My son loved the balcony. In his mind, anybody who sat in the balcony had the best seat in the house.

Glad to see that my son had been listening to me, but perplexed by his idea, I asked, "What do K and G stand for?" He wasn't a good speller yet. He was spelling phonetically. He said, "Dad! The KG balcony is for the *K*atholics and the *G*ews so they'll have the best seat in the house."

In the history of the Church, we have often closed off the balcony to people unlike us, reserving the best seats for ourselves and people like us. The Church's treatment of Israel—by which I mean the Jewish people, not the Jewish state—is perhaps the most shameful example of this exclusiveness. But as the authors of this book point out, Israel is both the root and fruit of the Church.

Israel is the *root* of the Church. God's blessing flows through Abraham and his descendants to the entire world (see Gen 12:1-3), finding its fulfillment in Jesus Christ (see 2 Cor. 1:19-21). We Gentile believers are grafted into the root of God's promises to them (see Rom. 11:17-18 NIV). Anti-Semitism in any form destroys the root of our faith.

Israel is also the *fruit* of the Church, though. At the present time, the majority of Jewish People may not believe in *Yeshua haMashiach*, but Paul prophesies that they will as the Second Coming draws near. "All Israel will be saved" (see Rom. 11:26). How? Through the Church's verbal witness to *"the power of God for the salvation of everyone who believes: first for the Jew, then for the Gentile"* (Rom. 1:16 NIV). Failure to witness to anyone, but especially the Jewish people, makes rotten the fruit of our faith.

The Church demonstrates her love for Israel and the world by her witness of the Gospel to them. But the Church's witness to the Gospel is not merely verbal. It is also social. God reconciles us to Himself through Jesus Christ, but He also reconciles us to one another at the same time. *"For [Jesus Christ] Himself is our peace, who has made the two [Jew and Gentile] one and has destroyed the barrier, the dividing wall of hostility.... His purpose was to create Himself* **one new man** *out of the two, thus making peace..."* (Eph. 2:14-15).

In Messiah Yeshua, Jews and Gentiles are not two people but one. Imagine the peace that would result in the Church and the world—and even in the Middle East!—if Christians simply preached and practiced the Gospel of Jesus Christ. In God's kingdom, the KG Balcony is open, and there's room for all.

George O. Wood
CEO and General Superintendent
of the Assemblies of God

The Identity of the One New Man

by Robert F. Wolff, Majestic Glory, President

One New Man is the name given to us by the Lord God. The vast majority of His Children have yet to awaken to this identity. Few are familiar with the term *One New Man,* or even know its whereabouts within the Scriptures. Yet there it stands in the fifteenth verse of the second chapter of Ephesians in all its glory.

> *For He Himself is our peace, who has made both one, and has broken down the middle wall of separation, having abolished in His flesh the enmity, that is, the law of commandments contained in ordinances, so as to create in Himself* **one new man** *from the two, thus making peace, and that He might reconcile them both to God in one body through the cross, thereby putting to death the enmity* (Ephesians 2:14-16.

What a remarkable statement concerning God's plan for peace and reconciliation between the two (Jews and Gentiles). Here is His expressly pronounced purpose: To bring all humanity together as One to magnify His Name. The world may have its own methods of pursuing unity, but none will succeed; unity can only be achieved in the acceptance of our God-ordained identity and destiny in *Yeshua HaMashiach* (Jesus the Messiah), God's own Son. This is God's design, and any other attempt will crumble as surely as the Tower of Babel. Bold words. God's words.

In the absence of finding our identity in the One sent by God, all humanity will simply adapt to its own culture and adopt its own chosen identity. Finding a place of our own making may give us a sense of familiarity and security, but it cannot achieve God's peace or His unity. This will only be accomplished God's way—in, through, and by Him, our Messiah Jesus.

What a blessing to know that all divisive strife stemming from humanly devised religious requirements and man-made stipulations has been overcome by Yeshua, the Lamb of God, on His tree of sacrifice. Through this act of supreme love, the dividing wall between the Jewish people and all other peoples and nations has tumbled. He is our peace.

All too often the Body of Believers loses sight of who we are. These marvelous Scriptures in Ephesians are the Lord's clarion call, reminding us that all redeemed humanity is One in Messiah. For nearly two millennia, we have divided the Body by pulling apart from one another. Disregarding the rich benefit of diversity in the myriad expressions of our faith, different strands of disciples have strained the boundaries of unity that our Lord fervently prayed for the night before He was crucified (see John 17).

The Lord is showing us the need for all believers to answer His call to be One. Gentile believers are to embrace and partner with believing Jewish people to fulfill our common God-given destiny as those called together by a new name: *One New Man*.

The book of Ephesians reveals the mystery that Jews and Gentiles are yoked together as joint heirs in the commonwealth of Israel (see Eph. 2:11-13). This fellowship of all citizens with the saints under the Lordship of Yeshua is transformed into a holy temple, the dwelling place of God in the Spirit (see Eph. 2:19-22).

Biblical history presents irrefutable evidence that God's Majestic Glory is poured out when God's Chosen Ones come together as *One New Man*.

Consider Joseph and Pharaoh, Joshua and Rahab, Esther and Ahasueras, Boaz and Ruth, Daniel and Nebuchadnezzer, and Peter and Cornelius—to name but a few. Jew and Gentile, every pair. These biblical couplings mark specific manifestations of God's saving grace that unquestionably altered the course of Israel and redirected God's designated plan for the salvation of His Chosen Ones, Jew and Gentile. When the children of Israel and the redeemed children of the Nations join as One in Israel's King-Messiah Yeshua, the power that God releases simply staggers the imagination.

The Lord has not hidden His plans from us. They are there for us to read, honor, and receive. Paul recounted Elijah's encounter with God as the Apostle prepared the hearts of the Romans, both believing Jews and Gentiles, to be grafted into Israel's patriarchal olive tree as a clear demonstration of *One New Man*. Today, as in those days, God keeps His remnant on call.

When all believers walk together in this *One New Man* identity, we fulfill the calling of our King. As we all receive and embrace one another so as to walk in the fullness of the identity given to us by God Himself—Jewish people and Gentiles, One in Messiah— the world will see and understand the time is near for the Second Coming of Yeshua, our Messiah. The Lord is looking for a bride that has prepared herself for His Return.

Our identity is in our Messiah, not in ourselves. This is our Lord's astonishing gift to us. Walking together as *One New Man* is the absolute, undeniable testimony that the walls of division between His Chosen Ones have been broken down, so the world would believe Yeshua HaMashiach is the One God promised Moses would return looking for His remnant.

Assembled before you are 12 noteworthy authors, gathered as *One New Man* to teach us about our true identity. They come together as One for the purpose of guiding us His Ways. We invite you: Absorb their words. Acknowledge the calling on your life. Accept the mantle set apart for you. Advance to the front. Announce His great love to all. Awaken the *One New Man*.

"Sh'ma, Yisra'el! ADONAI Eloheinu, ADONAI echad!"

"Hear, O Israel! ADONAI our God, ADONAI is one!"

(Deuteronomy 6:4)

CHAPTER 1

Allowing the Spirit to Refocus Our Identity

Dr. Jack W. Hayford, King's University, Chancellor

I, therefore, the prisoner of the Lord, beseech you to walk worthy of the calling with which you were called, with all lowliness and gentleness, with longsuffering, bearing with one another in love, endeavoring to keep the unity of the Spirit in the bond of peace. There is one body and one Spirit, just as you were called in one hope of your calling (Ephesians 4:1-4).

Among my most treasured moments in ministry have been occasions I have been invited to serve as a spokesperson for reconciliation between fellow Christian believers whose ethnicity has historically presented obstacles for many of each group to withdraw from the other. I have been privileged to speak in settings where due diligence was being shown by both sides of an historic ethnic barricade. Such cases included me in ministering as a team member of settings involving (a) American black and white males, (b) Native or "First" Americans (North

American Indians) and U.S. citizens of European extraction, and (c) walking with several denominations who, together, confronted their respective group's involvement in racial bigotry, but now were coming to repentance and biblical brotherhood.

Unforgettable among these is that highlight occasion I shared with more than 1,000 leaders who were at the 2004 conference conducted by *The Road to Jerusalem* ministry led by Bill McCartney and Raleigh Washington. Dr. Bill Hamel and I each spoke, representing the historic and evangelical Christian community of our day, addressing Daniel Juster and Jonathan Bernis of the Messianic Jewish community. Our purpose was to break down all walls that have separated us as brothers within the One New Man.

Pastor Hamel and I were humbled to stand as representatives of Gentile believers, as well as Protestant denominational leaders, to pray as intercessory penitents for the violations—unintended or intentional—that have been inflicted by Gentile believers upon both the Jewish people historically and the Messianic Jewish brethren and sisters in recent years. We united on the platform, a large crowd comprising both peoples in near equal numbers. Though a symbolic act to those unaware of the spiritual power of "representational repentance," we invoked God's blessing to multiply our manifest unity of that moment in ever widening circles—among churches, groups, and individual believers globally.

In that moment, all who were present saw a living demonstration of the One New Man, Jew and Gentile grafted together, laying aside their differences, humbly asking forgiveness after centuries of persecution directed towards each other. Similar occasions in today's global Church evidence increasing openness to this and other points of necessary mutuality, of growing unity, and at other times of frank, humbling repentance or honest recanting of erroneous concepts that, having been embraced, "brace up" walls of separation.

The Lord Jesus is calling us now, to a broader and even deeper awareness and awakening—to a distinct arena of unity and oneness that cannot be neglected without missing our call to this twenty-first-century hour. It is *that*—the times—that mandate the Church rise with spiritual passion and action, and embrace the truth and practice inherent in the words of Ephesians 2, calling believing Jews and Gentiles to give place to our Lord's desire to platform "One New Man"—one *truly united* Body, fit for ministry, spiritual warfare, and servant-like compassion across our world—everywhere.

Needed: A Breaking, Not a Brilliance

I am honored to be invited to contribute to this collection of articles regarding the need for and pathway to a Body-wide awakening of the whole Church to God's purpose regarding the One New Man He intends to manifest through Christ Jesus—*Yeshua haMashiach*. It is also humbling to rehearse what, for my part, is more of a testimony than an exposition. My offering here is not to describe a brilliance of biblical insight that brought me my own awakening, but rather, how graciously the Holy Spirit "broke in." He began breaking away the cataracts of unperceived blindness and began processing my perspective in that way He grants a grace gift of revelation—a sudden insight that fully aligns with God's Word, but ignites understanding that exceeds your own, and puts you on track with increasing enlightenment as you study further.

As a pastor, I've always been a serious student, deeply committed to teaching my flock. As a Bible college and seminary professor, I've sought to anchor myself and my teaching in the Word, and the doctrine. In other words, I knew the Scriptures, but I must honestly say with an unaffected humility, I did not learn or come to discern what has been a "biblically and theologically sound" pathway of understanding and fellowship in regard to those distinct points of biblical understanding that help us relate to and minister regarding Messianic Judaism. (In passing, let me note that our seminary at The King's University now offers an accredited doctoral studies program in Messianic Jewish Leadership.)

Three Motivating Reasons to Write

What follows is an explanation of "how I got from there to here," that is, from where my past perspectives and experience were almost completely absent of any sense or need to think about or be open to this subject, to the sense of gratitude for and clarity of conviction I have today. Here, I have gone to considerable length and detail, beginning with three reasons explaining what motivates my lengthier testimony as it relates to my own God-graced introduction to and my approach in partnering with Messianic Jews.

The *first* reason is to assert that this has vastly enlarged my understanding of the Jewish world—an important fact, given the location of the Kings, as well as my pastoral base for the 31 years where I led and fed the congregation of The Church On The Way in Los Angeles. I hold *all Jews* in deep respect, no matter what their spiritual convictions may be. My belief is that our primary mission as a local congregation as well as an educational center training leaders for ministry in today's Church, is to love, affirm, and stand with the Jewish people and Israel, especially at this politically strife-filled season of history.

Knowing God's Word and discerning His ways of reaching to touch the hearts of His ancient chosen people is important to every one of us who see Jesus as the Messiah. Representing God's heart for them with supporting love and in relationship that reveals a generous spirit has proven to be a fruitful, trust-building approach; one I believe is consistent with the Spirit of Jesus.

The *second* reason is to indicate my agreement that every effort should be bent toward helping the whole Body of Christ recognize, embrace, and receive Messianic Jews with understanding. Their salvation in Christ is *not,* as some critics argue, based on a compromised theology. Their use of terminology uniquely descriptive of themselves as Jews and not as Christians is not a denial of Jesus Christ (*Yeshua haMashiach*, in Hebrew). Neither is their continuance in their cultural celebrations of the Jewish background an addendum to salvation by faith through grace alone, rooted in Christ and independent of the law or its rituals.

For this reason, soundly based Messianic believers not only deserve the embrace of the whole Body of Christ, they *need* it. The historic societal rejection of Jews in general, beside the distinct and sometime brutal rejection or persecution many experience after receiving Yeshua as Lord, absolutely mandates the sensitive understanding and warmest embrace by the whole Body of Christ. Understanding the biblical call to our relating with them as One New Man is a pivotal assist toward living this way.

The *third* reason is to express my belief that the truth and spirit essential to embrace the biblical call to the One New Man will only *ultimately* be received by a Holy Spirit-begotten awakening of a Gentile believer's "inner man." Reasoned teaching is valuable, but prayerful availability to the Holy Spirit, as the One Jesus said would "lead you into all truth," will determine the depth and practical commitment anyone brings to a One New Man lifestyle.

This is not because the subject is without intellectual or theological footings, but because it is *spiritual* truth. It will only realize a passionate response in our lifestyle where *hearts* invite the Holy Spirit—as they prayerfully open the Word and openly engage conversation and fellowship with Messianic leaders. This reality is not distinct for other "basics" about the transmission of transforming truth. For example, *not one of us* as Gentile believers *came* to Christ and unto new birth without the Holy Spirit's assistance— *none of us* were *reborn* by mental powers but by the Spirit's work of grace. And so it is that the nature of the theme at hand requires this same dependency upon Him.

A Spiritually Essential Precursor

The quest for One New Man—for acknowledging, pursuing, and embracing this spiritually essential precursor of God's *"last days spiritual awakening and awaiting worldwide revival"* (see Rom. 11:12,15,25)—must become an essential, vital to us, in us and through us all. It is critical because the Word of God exhorts us to pursue it. But today it is also at a crisis point of needed awakening in the living Church; remembering the times call for it—both *past times* as well as today's *unfolding times.*

Referencing the past—Gentile believers must give themselves to avoid the Church reliving any part of the sordid history of failure we servants of Jesus of Nazareth have written across the centuries as "Christians" relating to, or more frankly for the most part, *failing* the Jews. Those times *past* cannot be casually dismissed, especially at this early hour of the twenty-first century, when everything around us seems to warrant considering the possibility that we are living at the time the writer of Hebrews cites:

> *See that you do not refuse Him who speaks...whose voice then shook the earth; but now He has promised, saying, "Yet once more I shake not only the earth, but also heaven." Now this, "Yet once more," indicates the removal of those things that are being shaken, as of things that are made, that the things which cannot be shaken may remain. Therefore, since we are receiving a kingdom which cannot be shaken, let us have grace, by which we may serve God acceptably with reverence and godly fear* (Hebrews 12:25-28).

Thus, we reference the unfolding present—the tumultuous world in which you and I are called to leadership in Christ's/Messiah's Body.

Without question, these are days our identity as committed believes in Jesus Christ mandates our clarity of self-understanding concerning our relationship with Christ our Lord, and what *He* expects of our relationship with our Jewish brethren, as well as our understanding and support for all Jews globally and discerning support for Israel in her crises. These are times that born again believers in Jesus Christ, the Jewish Messiah, must be readied with a moral will to stand together in support amid a world being poisoned daily by a rapid and rabid increase in both anti-Semitic and anti-Christian actions and rhetoric. To do this, as believers in God, His Son, and His Word, we need to reevaluate our presuppositions—essentially to sift out the superficial in order to more firmly live out these times with deeply founded convictions.

So it is, in the light and spirit of the above, I invite you to join me as I relate the *essence*—a brief distillation—of a pilgrimage, of sorts; one that provides an account of one man's "awakening"— mine! As I write to both Gentiles and Jews, hoping to prompt all to seek a fuller discovery of their identity as One New Man, my choice has been to maintain brevity. My goal is to provide outlined points of understanding that my own biblically based spiritual awakening brought me. At the same time, I want to assure the reader that my growth in living out this lifestyle unquestionably had seasons of slow growth, with only gradual gains in understanding.

But the journey is worth the "stretching" it brings, not only because it is a biblically directed pursuit but also because of the *benefits* one may realize. I readily affirm, for my part, how thankful I am as I continue to realize ever-expanding relationships with wonderful people, both among unbelieving as well as believing Jews. I know that without the quest urged in this book you hold, I would otherwise never have found so warm a welcome or such enjoyable relationships with so many in the entire Jewish community.

My Awakening—Two Points via Parallels

I begin by drawing parallels between my experience and that of two people in the Bible. The first is the man Jesus healed who had been born blind. The second is Peter, whose response to the Holy Spirit occasioned the first step that eventuated in the early Church finding its way to understand its mission to the Gentiles—to the nations of the world.

I have already noted my belief that the Holy Spirit's touch of "revelation" must enable all of us to see the truths held in the Word of God. I am not implying a "mystical" approach to the Bible is essential; I am announcing that a tactical or analytical approach may often prove ineffective, though not because it is insincere. It is a valid but awkward statement to make that even in our approach to the Scripture it is sadly easy to step outside the bounds of sound interpretation.

First Corinthians 2:7-16 clearly declares this truth as we see how the "spiritual" is contrasted with the "natural" mind, and carefully discern that the latter is not automatically inactive at times, simply because a person has been born again. New birth most certainly capacitates us for "spiritual" understanding. But it is equally true that the revealing, teaching ministry of the Holy Spirit is only functional in the absence of personal prejudice, intellectual pride, or a disposition to entertain sin in one's life. Since each of us is subject to being tempted to any of those, we are wise to pray that God would prepare our hearts, to draw us to genuinely humble availability to "see" our identity in His One New Man. These words hold a biblical proposition with a spiritually enriching possibility for each of us—indeed, for all the Church at large! It is a wonderful, highly livable and relational prospect for the Christ's/Messiah's Body, made possible by our Savior's life-gift of salvation for the whole world—for the Jew first and also for the Gentile.

The Man Born Blind

First, my "awakening" was a process similar to the experience of the man "born blind." Just as the man whose eyes Jesus "anointed" with mud and then commanded him to go and wash in the pool of Siloam, I was alive—literally and spiritually. But other than a general understanding of "the Jews and Israel in last days prophecies," I had no perception of the implications of the last days involving an unveiling of Jews to their Messiah *before* the Church was "taken up" to be with Christ. Though "born again" (like the blind man was physically alive) I was introduced by God's grace to a progressing understanding of the Word of God as it pertains to the Jews in our times—and increasingly to see what it called for in my response.

It is an interesting study to elaborate at greater length, however, briefly observe here with me how his "seeing" was first, entirely achieved by Jesus' sovereign act, initiating the man's ability to see visually. But second, it processed to his seeing more deeply with time, as progressive understanding followed an initial unveiling. Moving through John 9, the Bible shows the man proceeding from the miraculous recovery of his eyesight, to an increasing discovery of who Jesus was.

With his first answer to the question, "How were your eyes opened," he described his limited perception of Jesus only as *"a man"* (verse 11).

Next, to the Pharisee questioning him as to, "What do you say about him?" the man said, *"He is **a prophet**."*

The third inquiry—a further grilling by the religious leaders—occasions his great statement, "One thing I know—once I was blind but now I see!"

The interaction continues from there (verse 25) to his conclusion that his Healer was *"a man from God."*

Finally, when Jesus personally seeks out the man (verses 35-38), we see the Savior escort him unto full understanding of Himself as *"the Son of God."*

#1 —A Parallel Re: Progressing Realization

Parallel to the man born blind: I was "born again" already but was "blind" to the truth of the principle that reveals the *spiritual* indebtedness *all* believers owe to the Jews (see Rom. 15:15-17). Though I had received Christ, as well as having received His call into pastoral ministry before I entered college, I was in pastoral ministry nearly 15 years before I began to see how unaware I was. The implications of my spiritual obligation to prioritize our call to *first,* love, honor and thus *reach out* to God's ancient people, the Jews. I was "blind though born again," not even "seeing" the many basic biblical statements that forthrightly reveal that my faith in Jesus Christ had brought me (a) through *their* promised Messiah (see Gal. 3:26-27), (b) into an intended unity *with believing Jews* in the Body of Christ (see Gal. 3:28), (c) uniting us with them in faith first seeded by *Abraham* (see Gal. 3:29) and, (d) by faith in Christ alone, apart from the law, *grafting me* into the single root system through which eternal life flows—from the Messiah (see Isa. 53:2-6).

Simon Peter's Vision at Joppa

The account of Peter's experience in Acts 10 records a second picture somewhat parallel to my "awakening" to the truth of God's One New Man hopes for all the redeemed. Opening to that passage, it is clear that Peter was, in yet another way, "blind" until the Holy Spirit confronted and enlightened him to truth fully revealed in the Scriptures all the time. His eyesight was not his problem, but his scope of vision for Gentiles was blocked by tradition.

Peter's awakening came about by, and probably required, a vision that was deeply disturbing. It was a shocking vision—one that drastically upset his sensitivities. As he beheld it, distaste and embarrassment flooded his mind and emotions as God presented him with a bewildering scene of unclean and creeping creatures. He was presented with an array of animals and insects; all of which were previously forbidden by God as being unfit for consumption by His people of covenant.

Then his encounter cuts to the core of all he had been taught as the Holy Spirit commands him, "Rise, Peter, kill and prepare these unclean creatures for dinner." The command, at first seeming to introduce "false doctrine," was not reversing God's Word, but shaking him awake to God's fuller call to His will. Peter was brought to the amazing discovery that his "doctrine of separation" regarding impurity had blinded him to God's desire to beget a redeemed people—Jews *and Gentiles!—united* in truth and love, now equally granted God's grace and authority as "His people." The result of his awakening was the opening of the young Church to its mission to the Gentiles; a mission to bring them "in"—into a circle, a communion that he until that day thought reserved for Jews only (see Acts 10-11, 15).

#2 — A Parallel Re: Cultural Separatism

Peter could not even imagine seeing Gentiles becoming followers of Jesus without becoming "Jews" in ritual practices according to the Old Testament Mosaic systems. In short, being "saved" meant, "become a Jew." The call was to a salvation linked to *duties/rituals* (works) more than *faith*. And Peter, though bold in his commitment to the Lord, represented an entire culture that did not "see" the greatness of God's intent.

Then came His vision in Joppa, as the Holy Spirit invaded an unwittingly prejudiced man's prayer closet to overthrow Peter's presumed correctness regarding his cultural separatism from Gentiles. Again, a stream of experiences—a process—establishes a new perspective. His transformation begins with his spiritual encounter in Joppa (see Acts 10:9-16); the sudden and surprising confirmation of the arrival of the men sent to invite him to come to a Gentile home is attended by the Holy Spirit's directive: "Go with them—nothing doubting." But this is only the beginning.

The whole of the report in Acts 10-11 is a study in what can happen when *only one* leader allows the Holy Spirit to reveal God's will for His people to break through cultural separatism. The outcome manifest in Peter's experience is a testimony to what each of us can expand in the Body of all today's believers. To see our identity in the Spirit's biblically given "vision" of the One New Man calls us to grow in obedience as a people of attitudinal reconciliation; mutually practicing life-to-life integration, and growing with a dynamic witness to practical spirituality in the eyes of a watching world as we live in unity and partnership.

It begins with a heart being opened, just as Peter opened his, and advances as the Spirit of God processes hearts like ours from step to step. We saw it in Parallel #1, and it is here in its own unique expression in Parallel #2: (a) Peter's vision, (b) Peter's will to travel to a Gentile home, (c) God's amazing confirmation of His power and love toward Gentiles as Peter obeys, (d) Peter's forthright report and the response by the apostles in Jerusalem, (e) their collective choice to send Barnabas to see God's works among Gentiles in Antioch, and (f) the reciprocal support gift of the Antioch Church to Jews for famine relief in Jerusalem.

The whole sequence is a lesson, shouting to us: *If any one of us—but better, each* one of us—will open to the Lord's purpose to give rise to One New Man, revival will spread and Messiah Jesus will be glorified through His Church! Peter's vision in Joppa, obediently responded to, instigated an awakening among first-century believers that not only opened the doors of acceptance to Gentiles but also set in motion the global spread of the Gospel.

Our Reverse Ways re: Parallel #2

Peter's "blocked vision" prior to this event manifested in a Jewish mindset that couldn't imagine God working among the Gentiles—much less, that He would expect them to bond as one with them. For me, until the transforming process began in the early 1970s, *I could not have imagined seeing Jews open to their Messiah as it has happened over recent decades!*

Gradually, the Holy Spirit confronted me with my need for adjustment—for being processed by increasing calls to "stretch" as far as God's arms of love do, to embrace people with whom I had virtually no association at all. The summons to let God work His heart for His people in me effected changes in my perspective and adjustments in how I ministered. Perhaps one of the most dramatic examples was my being brought to think through the very term, *Christian* and what it did and didn't mean—how it had confused and how it had abused.

I met Jewish believers in Yeshua who still called themselves Jews and said it was counterproductive to say they had become Christian. I came to understand the challenges they faced in distinguishing their "new birth" and commitment to Jesus as Messiah as something very different from two presuppositions essential to avoid as they bear witness: (1) Coming to Yeshua (Jesus) was not an entry into a system with a sordid history of persecuting and killing Jews—a sorry fact of "Christian" behavior over past centuries. Further, (2) receiving the Messiah—Yeshua of Nazareth as revealed in the New Testament—was not a rejection of their ethnic Jewishness.

However, misunderstandings regarding these issues have constituted a problem for many evangelicals who fault Messianic Jews for this choice, notwithstanding the reality of the Jewish believers' testimony to their salvation; fully according to Acts 13:38-39. Though they have openly confessed Jesus as Savior (i.e., in Yeshua haMashiach), they are kept, in a sense, in the "outer court," separate from a trusted welcome to fellowship.

It is a peculiar—and very painful—reversal of the precise attitude that many Jews in the early Church held toward Gentiles who had been born again but did not observe part of the ceremonial requirements in Old Testament law. Just as there was a separate court on the Temple grounds, confining Gentiles to limited integration with Jews, the Church today is parsed in part by some who hold Messianic Jews at a distance. (Sadly, such separatism is not only common among believers in this one regard: supposed "superior revelation" or "more excellent insight," though declining in dramatic ways today, regrettably still imposes its presence between other groups of believers as well.)

Consider the possibility that our call to the One New Man, if responded to, may very conceivably be the key to the whole Body of Messiah opening to one another! Even though Peter, as a Jew, avoided Gentiles at the start, his receptivity of the Holy Spirit's call beyond his until-then-unperceived sectarianism opened the door to a breakthrough that set the stage for the New Testament to truly receive and activate the call Jesus gave to "go to all nations."

Allow me to begin drawing a conclusion to my testimony, with my humble appeal to all believers in Yeshua Adonai (the Lord)—Christ Jesus our Savior—by offering one illustration that describes just one "Christian" habit that God in His providence helped me to see and adjust. It was a very practical discovery of my own dependence on a "cultural approach" that was an example of mistaking wherein our identity as believers rests. Let me relate it as one case of a personal lesson I learned en route to understanding the Word's call to One New Man.

First, let me say it clearly: I am not ashamed to be called a "Christian!" However, the pilgrimage I'm relating brought me to see that the Word of God had never assigned me the mission of preaching "Christianity," and that neither did the Scriptures *anywhere* command people to "become a Christian" to be saved. God's Word says. "Believe on the Lord Jesus Christ and you will be saved."

At first I wrestled with this question about a treasured, traditional word. However, I recognized God's simpler appeal not only reached with a sensitivity to *all* peoples, and now, for over 35 years, having resolved this issue in the Scriptures, I invite people to acknowledge their repentance and their will to turn to the Lord God, our Maker and Creator, to receiving Jesus, His Son as their Savior. A typical invitation may sound like this:

> "He's the Lord," I say: "He died for our sins to bring us to Father God, He rose from the dead to prove He's who He says He is, and no one comes to the Father but through Him. His love invites you to come home to Him—How do you receive His love? Listen, 'God so loved the world, He gave His Son.' Do you hear that—the way to receive God's love is to receive His Son, Jesus. I'm not asking you to receive a religion, I'm inviting you to open your heart to Jesus—to Yeshua—the Savior—the Messiah."

I had been blind to the way that "Christian" presented a "call to a culture," rather than a call to the Person—Jesus our Savior, the Messiah and Lord of all. Among other things, I realized that this same blindness was not only a block to what became clearer communication to *people of any culture* I might address in Jesus' name. However, the point is that it helped me avoid an insensitivity that would be counterproductive to speaking with sensible and spiritual sensitivity in any setting where evangelical Christians were seen as opposed to Jews in general, or unkindly disposed toward Messianic Jews. Of course, I want to encourage Jewish believers in Yeshua as Savior in their walk with Him...and with all their spiritual brothers and sisters of Gentile background.

So this chapter gives something of a testimony and a teaching, if it might be received as such. It reflects my great love and respect for Jews on any terms. However, I want to convey my distinct desire to honor each Jewish person whom the *Ruach haKodesh* (the Holy Spirit) has brought to faith in Jesus of Nazareth as the Son of God, Savior. They represent the people God chose millennia ago to bear the testimony of the One God, Creator of all, to deliver the Holy Scriptures to the world, and to be the avenue by which the world's Redeemer, the Son of God, would be born. In a very real sense, each of them may well be acknowledged as my "elder brothers and sisters," and thereby I pursue the unity of our fellowship in Yeshua. Together, we have humbled ourselves before God's love and grace through Jesus Christ, and have "come back to the true and Living God—Yahweh; the God and Father of our Lord Jesus Christ; *Abba Yahweh*—the God of Abraham, Isaac and Jacob, the Rock of Israel; the God of the Bible's old and new covenant and the King of the Universe!

So it is that as I look back, I am repeatedly reminded that only the Holy Spirit could have gotten through to register the truths and the understanding I now treasure. I do not value it as though I felt it a private possession, but as a "releasing wealth" that awaits every believer. Further, I in no way feel myself "somehow accomplished" as an advocate today for unity in the Body of Christ or as one who "really understands" Messianic Judaism. I neither claim that now, nor do I ever feel I'll *master* anything of God's consummate wisdom. For my part, it's simply enough to submit myself to the *"mastery of the Master."* With His help and His Holy Spirit's promptings along the way, I want to live out my part in *all* Jesus has for me, including my being faithful to answer to this moment's demands in relating to Christ's One New Man.

CHAPTER 2

The One New Man in John 17

Dr. Raleigh B. Washington, Promise Keepers, President

I am convinced that the central core of the mysteries of heaven is contained in the high priestly prayer of Jesus, and I am mystified that so few pay close attention to our Lord's intentions.

The irrefutable truth running through the prayer of Jesus is that the power of unity, specifically between Jewish and Gentile believers, is the key to unlocking the mystery of the Kingdom of Heaven. Why is it that we, the Church, ignore this powerful truth?

John 17 presents the longest and most profound prayer of our Lord recorded in Scripture. We have the privilege of witnessing, through the eyes and ears of the disciples, this intimate conversation between God and His only begotten Son.

As Jesus spoke to the Father, He acknowledged that He had accomplished the work that His heavenly Father had given Him to do. Having achieved His purpose, Jesus requested the glory that He had with the Father before the world existed. He recounts His accomplishments, specifically that He has revealed the Father to

His disciples, and then He prays for their protection as they carry on the work He came to establish.

The prayer then reveals the core purpose and accomplishment of the incarnation of Jesus. He had emptied Himself of His glory. He had become like man in every way except the curse of sin, to achieve the central mystery of the Kingdom of Heaven—to redeem lost mankind and establish the One New Man, the Body of Messiah, the Bride of Christ.

By the mercy of God, we discover the centrality of this mission and the eternal importance of its fulfillment, as Jesus explains the reason why He prays for protection for His disciples. Jesus knows He is leaving this world and they are not going with Him.

We have here a peek inside heaven's realm and a glimpse of the Father's plan. If the only thing that concerned Jesus were His disciples' safety, He would have prayed for them to be removed from the world immediately. There could be no safer place than Heaven. But He did not pray for them to be taken out of the world. Instead, He clearly states His purpose: *"As you sent Me into the world, I also have sent them into the world"* (John 17:18 NASB).

In this single declaration, we have the essence of our commission as the body of Christ. We are sent into the world to proclaim the work of redemption accomplished by the Son of Man, Jesus the Messiah.

These and Those

The disciples would continue His work. The goal of that work is delineated as Jesus expands the scope of His prayer from "these" disciples to *"those also who believe in Me through their word."* The goal here is that "these" and "those" may all be one. This revealed mystery of unity would become the means by which the world would recognize that Jesus came from the Father.

I do not ask on behalf of these alone, but for those also who believe in Me through their word; that they may all be one; even as you, Father, are in Me and I in You, that they also may be in Us, so that the world may believe that You sent Me. The glory which You have given Me I have given to them, that they may be one, just as We are one; I in them and You in Me, that they may be perfected in unity, so that the world may know that You sent Me, and loved them, even as You have loved Me (John 17:20-23 NASB).

In these four verses, the entire scope of God's plan for His children is revealed in the most succinct statement anywhere in Scripture. He prays for perfected unity as a prerequisite to the fulfillment of His mission to reveal the Father to the entire world.

This prayer calls for a spiritual and physical oneness that must come to fruition *before Jesus will return* to claim His bride, the Body of Messiah, and present her holy and blameless before the throne of God.

The essence of this profound mystery of heaven is revealed in this prayer through the three things for which Jesus prays: power or fullness of glory (verses 1-5), protection of His disciples (verses 6-19), and perfection in oneness between Jewish and Gentile believers (verses 20-26).

The specificity of His prayer, to identify both Jew and Gentile in this oneness, is frequently missed by Gentile believers. They generally prefer to think of unity in broader terms of denominational cooperation or general racial tolerance. Notice the manner in which Jesus uses the word "glory." He prays for the powerful glory He had before the world was, yet He uses this glory to ensure permanent manifestations of a relational oneness between Jewish and Gentile believers. Why? This manifest oneness will catalytically cause the spiritual eyes of Jew and Gentile to be opened, and they will recognize and believe that Jesus (Yeshua) is the Messiah.

Do not miss it! This is the central mystery of heaven, which was hidden in past generations—the mystery of Christ!

> *You can understand my insight into the mystery of Christ, which in other generations was not made known to the sons of men, as it has now been revealed to His holy apostles and prophets in the Spirit; to be specific, that the Gentiles are fellow heirs and fellow members of the body, and fellow partakers of the promise in Christ Jesus through the Gospel* (Ephesians 3:4-6 NASB).

The Disciple's Prayer

Early in His ministry, Jesus introduced the idea of One New Man unity in a different setting. The Disciple's Prayer (often called the Lord's Prayer) in Matthew 6 incorporates not only a description of oneness between heaven and earth, but mandates reconciliation through forgiveness as the pathway to unity.

This prayer, as Jesus taught it to His disciples, requires that we discern the will of God, as it exists in heaven, and seek its manifestation here on earth. He then emphasizes the giving and receiving of forgiveness between disciples as a key element in establishing God's Kingdom. Jesus considers this so important that He expands on the subject at the end of the prayer.

> *For if you forgive others for their transgressions, your heavenly Father will also forgive you. But if you do not forgive others, then your Father will not forgive your transgressions* (Matthew 6:14-15 NASB).

This forgiveness is the foundation of maintaining oneness among followers of Jesus. Offenses between individuals not only create walls of hostility between each other but also obstruct our communication with God.

Apply this principle to Jewish and Gentile believers and you will see that it is the same message found in John 17:20-23 and in Ephesians 2:14-16. The will of God in heaven is evident in the oneness that exists between Father, Son, and Holy Spirit. This oneness represents the will of God on earth between all disciples, especially Jew and Gentile. As He prays, Jesus first acknowledges the vertical relationship between Father and Son; then He prays that this will be duplicated in the horizontal personal relationships exhibited between His followers "on earth as it is in heaven."

The mystery of the kingdom of heaven is revealed here in the teaching of the Disciple's Prayer. This is to be a consistent prayer of all disciples of the Messiah. The prayer for the kingdom of heaven to be manifest on earth reflects this relational oneness between believers. The point here is to recognize that Jesus prayed, in part, the same prayer He taught His disciples to pray. In essence, our Lord was teaching us: This is how we become the One New Man.

The Foundational John 17 Thrust

Everything in John 17 builds toward the central message contained in verses 20-23. The prayer is for relational oneness within the body of believers between Jew and Gentile. This oneness is to be modeled after the oneness in the Godhead (verse 21), causing the unbelieving world of Jews and Gentiles to gain faith and believe that Jesus is the Messiah, the One sent by God to fulfill His purposes. This oneness will open the eyes of the world, both instilling faith and satisfying the prerequisite for the return of our Lord.

Correct understanding of this passage requires a recognition that two categories of people are addressed in verse 20—Jew and Gentile. The apostle Paul, in Ephesians 2:14, reflects this same understanding by describing all believers as broken into these same two groups. He further recognizes the reality that these two groups have not gotten along. He uses the word "enmity" and describes the "barrier of the dividing wall." The New International Version translates this as "the dividing wall of hostility."

Paul does not leave the two divided, however. In the next two verses, he tells us that Jesus has destroyed the division and created from the two divided groups One New Man, reconciling them both "in one body to God through the cross." In this statement, we see the crucial importance of the atonement provided by the crucifixion of Jesus. Only because of the redemptive sacrifice of Yeshua is it possible for any of us to obtain forgiveness from the Father. And only after we are forgiven by the Father is it possible for us to forgive and to love others.

The One New Man describes our relationships within the body of Messiah. The totality of these relationships within the body of Christ is summed up by the words "both groups." Through his inspired words, Paul states that only two groups of people are identified by the Holy Spirit—Israel and the nations. If the dividing wall of hostility that existed between these two groups was destroyed by the work of Jesus at Calvary, then the world should observe a harmonious relationship between Jewish and Gentile believers. This will provoke unbelieving Jews to jealousy and further cause unbelievers, in general, to believe that Jesus is Messiah.

Why Two Groups—the Chosen and Everybody Else?

We might reasonably inquire why this division into two groups exists. Did not God Himself create it when He separated Israel from the rest of the nations, designating them as His chosen people?

We need to understand the importance of God's selection of the Jews. His plan did not involve hostility. He always intended the One New Man to be the reality of His people, both Jew and Gentile.

There is a spiritual reason for the identification of two groups of people by both John and Paul. The Old Testament also categorized people into two groups—Jews and foreigners (see 2 Chron. 6:32) God chose the Jews to be the vehicle through which He would save the world, to be a light to the nations, the Gentiles, and to be the people among whom He would place His Son to be Savior of the world. Jesus came for the lost sheep of the house of Israel (see Matt. 15:24). Jesus gave the Gospel to the Jews and commissioned them to take this Gospel to the world, that is, all the nations (*Ethnos, ethnics*; see Matt. 28:18-20).

Hence, the underlying reason for choosing Jewish people to be His very own people was to set into motion His plan for the salvation of the world; to establish a kingdom of believers on earth who would ultimately believe in His only begotten Son and obey all of His commandments, and to be the central expression of God's plan for the salvation of the world.

God chose a people to be His instrument for salvation, and this salvation is dependent on a *relationship* between all people, specifically Jew and Gentile. This relationship is to be an example of brotherly love (see John 13:34-35); a revelation of the mystery of the kingdom (see Matt. 13:11); an answer to His high priestly prayer (see John 17:20-22); and the epitome of peace in the kingdom (see Eph. 2:14-16).

God did not create the wall of hostility that has separated Jew from Gentile. That was our own doing. God intentionally separated the Jews from the Gentiles in order to bring the One New Man into being.

The One New Man

Several years ago, a respected national leader said that we should not use the phrase "One New Man" because most people would not know what we were talking about. This gesture was intended to be helpful to our ministry and to make it more relevant to where the Church is. Despite the fact that this concept is directly related to the redemptive work of Christ at Calvary, it is not taught by most of the Church. The apostle Paul tells us that one of the primary reasons for the death of Christ on the cross was to destroy the enmity between Jewish and Christian believers, creating One New Man.

Just as the second greatest commandment is equal to the first, so the second reason stated for Calvary by Paul, creation of the One New Man, must be elevated in priority within the Christian faith (see Matt. 22:34-40). Although the Bible is explicit in stating the first commandment, the Church often emphasizes, "to love God with all of our heart, mind and soul," and ignores "to love our neighbor as ourselves." Indeed, the manifestation of loving God first must be reflected in how and if we love our neighbor as ourselves. This is a part of the wondrous mystery of the kingdom made manifest through Jesus.

There is an irrefutable connection between the two greatest commandments, the high priestly prayer and the One New Man. The commandments that Jesus gave the highest priority were those that said to love God and to love each other. The high priestly prayer was for all who would believe to exhibit the same unity that Jesus has with His Father. The One New Man is portrayed as the unity resulting from the work of Jesus on the cross.

Biblically and theologically, all these passages carry the same message—they are all about relationships and portray the one-ness for which Christ died. Hence, First John 4:20 tells us that loving God and hating your brother can only mean you do not truly love God. Likewise, you cannot truly embrace His work of redemption and not embrace the second victory Jesus achieved at Calvary—destroying the dividing wall of hostility between Jewish and Gentile believers so that they would be *One*, resulting in peace in the kingdom of God.

We have already seen the One New Man demonstrated. The early church is an excellent example of oneness in kingdom relationships. Acts 2 tells us that no believer lacked anything he needed because all shared with one another based on need. Hence, the early church understood and responded to the prayer of our Lord in John 17, due in major part to the accurate teachings of His apostles, for whom He prayed.

The concept of the One New Man was a foundational part of the life of the Church even before the Church existed. Jesus specifically prayed for it, the early church manifested it, and Paul gave it a name. Considering the importance of this theme throughout the New Testament, we cannot ignore the One New Man just because the Church is unfamiliar with it. Rather, we need to study it and teach it and authoritatively proclaim it until the Church does know what we're talking about.

An unmistakable priority unfolds with Paul's teaching in Ephesians 2:14-16. He starts with Jesus as the embodiment of peace. Next he describes how Jesus fosters genuine peace between Jewish and Gentile believers, making them relationally *one* by destroying the dividing wall of hostility existing between the two groups. This represents a spiritual work that demands a physical result—Jewish and Gentile believers in Jesus to embrace each other in the model of the trinity (see John 17:21). Paul places equal importance on this relationship and the redemptive relationship with God for both groups, expressed in this very same passage. We must recognize that Paul is reiterating what Jesus prayed in John 17.

Some see this as a spiritual relationship only, based on the finished work of Christ on the cross. However, the relationship between God the Father, God the Son, and God the Holy Spirit is *both* spiritual and actual. Hence, the same is true for the One New Man. The spiritual relationship between Jew and Gentile believers is a done deal, completed by the finished work of Christ at Calvary.

The Calling

The physical relationship must be acted upon by each believer seeking the opportunity to connect across that destroyed wall of hostility between Jewish and Gentile believers, directly, indirectly, or by whatever means possible to demonstrate support, solidarity, and oneness. As we see the end time approaching, this unity becomes more important than ever. We are told in Zechariah 12 that the day will come when *every* nation will turn against God's chosen people.

The next goal in this priority sequence is the establishing of peace: It is preceded by the word "thus," meaning that the steps leading up to this point have systematically resulted in God's peace. Jesus, His finished work at Calvary, His prayer for oneness, and His command for oneness leave no doubt whatsoever that the visible relationship between Jewish and Gentile believers in Christ is the mystery of the kingdom. Nor can there be any doubt that every element of this sequence has been orchestrated by the Prince of Peace, yielding His perfect peace.

The oneness resulting in God's peace between the two groups, Jewish and Gentile believers, is applicable to all believers, regardless of ethnic identity. However, Paul intentionally identifies all believers in Christ under the demarcation of "two groups" for two significant reasons: (1) the pre-Calvary enmity between Jewish and Gentile believers was destroyed by the shed blood of Yeshua, and (2) this particular act reveals one of the primary purposes of God sending His Son into the world to reveal the mystery of the kingdom of God that was hidden in previous generations. This mystery reveals that Gentiles are fellow heirs, fellow members of the body, and fellow partakers of the promise in the Messiah through the Gospel (see Eph. 3:3-6). This is a cause for great celebration. Hallelujah!

Remember, Jesus Himself said that He came first to the lost sheep of the house of Israel, even though He informed them that

He had another fold—Gentiles (see John 10:16)—that would be added to make what we might well call One New Flock. The central truth in His high priestly prayer in John 17 emphasized this very fact. You cannot be connected to Jesus without being connected to Israel.

The Holy Spirit obviously deemed it necessary to reiterate this revealed truth of the kingdom through the apostle Paul in Ephesians 2. Although this truth involves a spiritual destruction of hostility between Jewish and Gentile believers, we must not overlook, as is the case with much of the body of Christ, the fact that a tangible *relationship* between these two groups is clearly intended. *Tangible* implies that we are close enough to talk, to touch, and to interact. Tangible oneness is an imperative behavior for those who would live as the One New Man.

The Greatest Harvest

The message of John 17 is clear. Jesus prayed, just as He had taught His disciples to pray, that relationships in the kingdom on earth would be as they are in heaven. He prayed for a visible unity that would reflect the unity of heaven. In relating the model of the relationship of the Trinity as the goal of relationships in the kingdom on earth, He displayed a singleness of divine intent for the two groups who were the subject of His prayer in verse 20, "these"—His Jewish followers—and "those"—the Gentiles who would believe through them. He prayed that they would reflect on earth a relationship that is mirrored within the Trinity. We dare not miss this directive.

Who would not consider what Jesus asks the Father to help facilitate as anything other than a manifesto—an unmistakable mandate for Jewish and Gentile believers? This is the core thrust of His prayer. It is so important to Jesus that He now gives the two groups, Jews and Gentiles, the very glory He had with the Father before the world began. He did this so that they would have the spiritual power to be one in tangible relationship with each other.

At least two factors make the unity of the One New Man critical for the Church. This relationship is the nonnegotiable key to causing the unbelieving world (both Jew and Gentile) to catalytically believe that Jesus is the "Sent One," the Messiah! This relationship is the biblical pathway to the worldwide harvest, and will heal the partial blindness of God's chosen people who rejected their Messiah.

The One New Man hastens the return of our Lord. In fact, this is no less than a prerequisite for Messiah's coming. Our Lord said He would not return until His people, the chosen Jews, recognized and accepted Him, reflected by their praise of thanksgiving: *"Blessed is He who comes in the name of the LORD"* (Matt. 23:39).

We must not miss the fact that Jesus gives the body of Messiah the responsibility to prepare the circumstances for His return. He also gives us the formula and procedure to successfully fulfill this responsibility. He does this in the context of linking the manifesto within the context of His compassionate prayer to the Father, interceding for all—Jew and Gentile—who would believe in Him.

We have been called to prepare the pathway for our Lord's return. He has shown us how to perform His will. We have received His manifesto within His priestly prayer of compassion, made before the presence of the His apostles. He has displayed His purpose that all who believe—Jews and Gentiles—will know that He was sent by God for our salvation.

This is our manifesto: to intentionally prepare the way for the return of Messiah Yeshua by actively seeking the unity of the One New Man, Jew and Gentile in the fulfillment of this High Prayer, as proclaimed by our High Priest.

CHAPTER 3

Discovering the Purpose of Our Identity as One New Man

Dr. Mitch Glaser, President, Chosen People Ministries

During my time as a student at Fuller Theological Seminary, I became acquainted with a retired and now deceased Fuller professor, Dr. Arthur Glasser. Dr. Glasser is a Gentile believer who especially loved two groups of people: the Jewish people and the Chinese. Dr. Glasser gave the first half of his life to reaching the Chinese (he was exiled from China at the rise of Mao) and the second half to missions education at Fuller Seminary, while at the same time doing all he could to promote the preaching of the Gospel among Jewish people.

He was a rare Gentile who, more than anybody I know, embodied the magnificent unity described in the text of Ephesians 2. Dr. Glasser tirelessly promoted Jewish evangelism and advocated for the reconciliation of Jews and Gentiles in the Body of Messiah.

It is in his honor that I submit the following reflections.

Brit, Bar Mitzvah, and Jesus

I was born in Brooklyn, New York, circumcised on the eighth day and raised in a typical New York City Jewish home. Both of my parents were Jewish, and like so many from the post-Holocaust generation, I grew up under the dark cloud of this cataclysmically tragic event. The result, at least for my family, was that we were profoundly anti-Christian and had little interaction with Gentiles/ Christians (in my understanding at the time) because we believed they had tried to destroy my people.

Like most Jewish young men, I was Bar Mitzvah[1] at the age of 13. I was sent to a modern Orthodox synagogue for Hebrew school and Bar Mitzvah training. The synagogue was more religious than my home, so I grew up with a degree of religious disparity from the very beginning. I could never quite connect with the Orthodox community because we were not religious at home and yet, my entire world was Jewish. I knew some non-Jews in school, but I grew up sensing a deep divide between myself, the community, and the "Gentile/Christian world."

The only interaction I really had with non-Jews was with the Italian and Irish Catholic kids as we battled over who had the right to use the local stickball courts. I was called "Christ-killer" many times growing up.

I cannot say that I actively hated or even disliked Gentiles/ Christians, but I knew we were something significantly "other" than they were. My attitude changed a bit when my family moved to New Jersey during my junior year of high school. I spent more time with Gentiles, but still found myself gravitating toward the Jewish kids. My family became more involved with a Conservative synagogue at that time, and I even played basketball in the Jewish basketball leagues.

I went off to college and became a "middle-class Jewish hippie," dropping out of college within my first semester and moving to San Francisco around the time of my eighteenth birthday. My best friends were fellow Jewish hippies like myself, but I was beginning to have closer non-Jewish friends as well. At this point in my life, the distinctions between Jews and Gentiles had become less relevant to me, as one of the values "hippies" held dear was the equality of all humanity.

Please do not mistake what I am saying. It is not that I stopped identifying as a Jew. Even as a hippie, I celebrated Passover, and I would never consider celebrating Christmas or Easter or setting foot in a church. The Gentile kids that were part of my small hippie community celebrated Christmas and Easter, but in a very irreligious way! In my understanding, "non-religious" Christians were similar to "non-observant" Jews and the distinctions between Jews and Gentiles were primarily cultural and ethnic, rather than religious. We never talked about these matters and essentially attributed our differences to our parents. We viewed religion as one of the problems that divided the humanity that we ideally wanted to unify.

My life began to change rapidly when one of my friends—a nice Jewish girl from the Bronx—became a believer in Jesus in the summer of 1970. My best friend, also a Jewish young man from the Bronx, became a believer in Jesus as well. Without prolonging the story, it did not take long before I, too, became a follower of Jesus in November of 1970.

When I became a follower of Yeshua, I knew there were non-Jews who believed in Him as well—but I had not met many at that time. I probably knew as many Jews who believed in Jesus as Gentiles who did. The Gentiles I knew who believed in Jesus did not have much to do with the more institutional church. They were mostly ex-hippies, and the unity we had in the past seemed to easily transfer as we became united in faith!

As I began meeting Gentiles who were part of the institutional evangelical church, I felt the old "gap" I had grown up with begin to widen. My Jewish identity and traditions began to matter more to me, now that I understood that being Jewish was connected to my faith in God and the Jewish Messiah. It seemed that Gentile believers (innocently) expected me to take part in Christian traditions and celebrations, but culturally these events felt very foreign.

I still remember a conversation I had with one young Gentile believer soon after I become a follower of Yeshua. We both attended a Thanksgiving meal and service in the Haight-Ashbury District of San Francisco. As I walked out he put his arm around me and said, "Mitch, if you think you enjoyed Thanksgiving—just wait until Christmas!"

I had so much hair on my head and on my face that he probably could not see that I turned completely red. I had no idea that by accepting Jesus I had seemingly exchanged my Jewish holidays for the "Christian holidays." I told him that I had not read that in the Bible!

I will admit that his statement—though well intentioned—caused me incredible trauma. It was my first brush with the identity issues I would face for the next 38 years as a believer, and still face to this very day.

In some ways, this is similar to marriage: I fell in love with my wife, also a Jewish believer, and wanted to marry her. It eventually dawned on me that I was not only marrying my wife, but also gaining a whole new family.

I quickly realized that I had not simply become a follower of Jesus the Messiah, but had also been invited to join His family, which included both Jews and a global variety of Gentiles. It was clear that I needed to better understand this new unity with my Gentile spiritual family members.

I am grateful for the text at hand in Ephesians 2, as this passage helps me understand God's will for me in my relationship to my Gentile brothers and sisters in the Messiah.

A Summary of the Text

Paul writes in Ephesians 2:14-16:

For He Himself is our peace, who has made both one, and has broken down the middle wall of separation, having abolished in His flesh the enmity, that is, the law of commandments contained in ordinances, so as to create in Himself one new man from the two, thus making peace, and that He might reconcile them both to God in one body through the cross, thereby putting to death the enmity.

I surmise that one of the reasons Paul penned the letter to the Ephesians was to express his concerns for the challenges faced by believers in both understanding and practicing their unity in the Messiah. Earlier in the chapter, Paul describes the position in Messiah that unites us and later illustrates in Ephesians 5, how husbands and wives, masters and servants, children and parents and, of course, Jews and Gentiles should live out this unity in everyday life. This unity is an answer to Yeshua's prayer in John 17 and evidently a deep concern of the Savior's heart.

Our passage teaches that peace—this new peace Jews and Gentiles share with one another—is found in the person of Jesus. He created peace by breaking down the "wall of enmity," through His death at Calvary. He did this, in my understanding, by making the exclusivity of the Torah[2] inoperative[3] (a better translation of the Greek than "abolished"), specified by the apostle as commandments, contained in ordinances[4] leading to the creation of One New Man.[5]

Certainly Paul, who in Romans 11:1 declared that he was still a Jew though he believed in Yeshua, is not suggesting that this New Man is the termination point for all ethnic identity. Rather, he is suggesting that when it comes to personal salvation, the Jewish people have no advantage over the Gentiles. He also affirms this in passages such as Galatians 3:28.[6] It is simply Paul's way of stating that the ground is level at the foot of the cross.

This is why he concludes this passage by reminding the believers in Ephesus that the end result of Jesus' work on the cross is peace between Jews and Gentiles—a microcosm of the Kingdom reconciliation, between nations, creation, and all facets of God's universe fragmented by sin (see 1 Cor. 15:28; Rom. 8:21-22), a reconciliation that will be fully manifested at His return.

We have peace and unity between Jews and Gentiles through Jesus, and the Torah that previously divided us now brings us together. The revelation of God's person and will for mankind, found in the Torah—through Jesus—belongs to both Jews and Gentiles. The exclusive right of the Jewish people to the Torah has been made inoperative without binding Gentiles to the Mosaic Covenant. In effect, because of Yeshua's death, Jews and Gentiles now share in God's promises to one another—non-Jews are brought near and Jewish believers in Messiah fulfill their calling as those who bless, intercede for, and reveal the One true God among the nations (see Gen. 12:3; Exod. 19:4-5; Isa. 43:10-11).

In the "One New Man," both Jews and Gentiles find their biblical destinies fulfilled. Yet I still believe the Scriptures teach that Jews and Gentiles retain their uniqueness within God's plan, and therefore we must not view the creation of this new entity as calling for the obliteration of differences created by God Himself. Rather, through the death of the Messiah, God has created a deeper and more profound unity between Jews and Gentiles in Jesus (see Eph. 3:6-7).

The One New Man and Jewish Identity

This "one new man" is the *ekklhsia*, the Church—those called out of this present world for God's holy and redemptive purposes. This new entity, built on the Jewish prophets and apostles (see Eph. 2:20), is also portrayed in the image of the olive tree in Romans chapter 11. Redeemed Jews and Gentiles are nourished by the same root (see Rom. 11:17) and "made to drink" of the same Spirit (see 1 Cor. 12:13).

Yet, I still wonder what the New Man sees when he looks in the mirror? I would suggest that the miracle of the One New Man is not that believers have lost their divinely appointed distinctions once they have become amalgamated into the Body of Messiah. Instead, the beauty of the New Man is that he has a composite identity expressed in perfect unity. I do not view these ongoing theological distinctions to be merely cultural, but actually to be biblically based. God's covenants with both Jews and Gentiles are ongoing and have been fulfilled, but not subsumed in the New Covenant. This only adds to the beauty of the One New Man—as unity is only supernatural when genuine distinctions exist.

I have often wondered why the One New Man is never portrayed as wearing a *yarmulke* (a skullcap often worn in prayer)? Why is he usually portrayed as a Gentile?

I have also found it odd that I was expected to embrace and celebrate "Christian holidays" when, from my vantage point, the Jewish holidays are more clearly specified in the Old Testament. In fact, in the New Testament we never find any passage commanding us to celebrate Christmas or Easter, but we find many passages in the Old Testament commanding the Jewish people to celebrate Passover, the Day of Atonement, the Feast of Tabernacles, etc. Jesus Himself observed these biblical festivals and there is still much to learn about our relationship with God in celebrating them—especially the festivals as fulfilled in Yeshua (see 2 Tim. 3:16).

Gentiles, who are part of the One New Man, draw closer to the biblical Jewish faith without becoming Jews or obligated to the Mosaic covenant. I believe the Apostle when he writes, *"But now in Christ Jesus you who once were far off have been brought near by the blood of Christ"* (Eph. 2:13).[7]

Perhaps from a biblical perspective, the One New Man should wear a metaphorical *yarmulke* and Messianic Jews should not be expected to remove theirs by embracing our more normative evangelical cultural expressions of the faith, especially in North America.

You Can Be Jewish and Believe in Jesus

When a Christian exhorts his Jewish friend to receive Jesus as Messiah, the Jewish person interprets what he hears as, "Would you like to give up your identity as a Jew and embrace the faith of those who persecuted your forefathers?"

Jewish people cannot easily understand that they can receive Jesus and remain Jewish. The two simply do not seem to fit together. As one Jewish man told me, "It is like eating a ham and cheese sandwich at a Bar Mitzvah!"

I recall the first time I took my mother to a Messianic Jewish worship service. My mom was not happy about my becoming a believer in Jesus! Finally, after almost ten years of trying, I coaxed her into going with me to a Messianic service. Mom stayed through the entire service, and I even gave the sermon that evening.

When I asked her afterward how she liked the service, she said what every good Jewish mother would say: "It was very nice." I probed a little further, asking what she thought of my message.

She responded, "You speak well, you should have been a lawyer." I asked what she though of the music, which was Messianic, and mostly in a minor key. She responded, "The music was wonderful and sounded very much like Jewish music." That should have been my tip-off as to where the conversation was headed. I said, "Mom, it sounded very Jewish because it is Jewish."

She looked at me and said, "Really?"

I said, "Yes."

She then asked the question, "So tell me, were any of these Jews baptized?"

I asked her, "What does that have to do with anything? After all, baptism is a very Jewish thing based on our *mikveh* and the cleansing rituals of Judaism."

She said, "If they were baptized, then they are no longer Jews, they are Christians." She repeated, "Aren't they Christians now?"

I said, "Yes, but they are still Jewish."

She responded, "That's impossible; once they are baptized they are no longer Jews."

I then said, "But, Mom—Jesus was Jewish, and even He was baptized, according to the New Testament."

She said, "Of course He was, everyone knows that Jesus converted to Catholicism!"

I did make some progress with my mom through the years, but it is still so very difficult for Jewish people to understand that a person can be Jewish and believe in Jesus. It is presumed within the Jewish community that a Jew who becomes a believer in Jesus has renounced his Jewish identity.

Our corporate testimony to the Jewish people is enhanced and empowered when Messianic Jews maintain some level of clear Jewish identification. In addition, when Gentile Christians show a deeper understanding and love for the Jewish people— the witness of the One New Man is made all the more powerful (see Rom. 11:11).

Some Familial Advice to My Gentile Brothers and Sisters

I know that most Gentile Christians would no longer encourage Messianic Jewish brothers and sisters to give up or downplay their Jewish heritage in order to accept Jesus. We do live in a glorious new day that is quite different from the time when I became a believer almost 40 years ago.

Yet we still have a distance to go! We must ask ourselves the question, "What can be done to strengthen our unity by affirming the mutual identities of our One New Man?" I am especially concerned with helping my Gentile brothers and sisters to encourage Messianic Jews who are part of local evangelical churches.

There are many ways to do this. First of all, encourage Jewish believers to remain Jewish and identify as Jews. It is psychologically unhealthy to deny a part of oneself, and we do little to enhance the witness of Jewish believers if they no longer identify as Jews.

Encourage your pastor to make mention of the Jewish festivals in your services. Celebrate Passover—why not? Jesus did! There is nothing more encouraging to the Jewish believer in your church than taking an interest in his or her Jewishness.

Encourage Jewish evangelism in your church. This will also show Jewish believers that you are interested in their families. Support Jewish missions. Take trips to Israel. Study the Old Testament Scriptures. Invite Jewish believers and missionaries to the Jews on a regular basis to be a part of your church services. The affirmation and encouragement Gentile believers offer to their Messianic friends can make an enormous difference to Jewish believers struggling with rejection by the greater Jewish community because of their faith.

In other words, it is a good idea to "put on a *yarmulke*" once in a while! As a Gentile believer, you will be a great blessing to the Jewish believers in your midst.

It is also important for Gentile believers to encourage the growth of our current Messianic movement. It is exciting to see so many Jewish people accepting Yeshua and continuing to identify as Jews.

There are now upwards of 350 Messianic congregations in North America and another 80 to 100 in Israel. There are also more than 100 in the former Soviet Union and dozens in Argentina, Germany, Brazil, and Australia.

I believe it would be a wonderful testimony for the Jewish community to see that true believers in Jesus cherish their Old Covenant heritage, recognize that the Savior of the world was born in a Jewish home and will one day return to reign in Jerusalem in His holy homeland.

Our unity, however, will be our greatest testimony to the world and to the Jewish community! I pray that this volume will encourage the One New Man across the globe to fulfill the vision of our Messiah who commanded His disciples love one another (see John 13:35).

Endnotes

1. Literally, a son of the commandment. This is the traditional rite of passage for a Jewish young man at 13 years of age.

2. The general term in Hebrew for Law is Torah. This refers both to the Five Books of Moses and also to the legislation given at Mount Sinai. This Law was given to the Jewish people, but even in Exodus 19, the Jewish people were called by God to mediate God's truth as priests to the Gentiles. This is why Israel was called to be a light to the nations. The purpose for God choosing the Jewish people was to bring the nations closer to the God of Israel—His Word, covenants, and promises.

3. The Torah, as a basis for division between Jews and Gentiles, is made inoperative. Through Jesus, Gentiles now have access to the Torah and the entirety of God's revelation without becoming Jews or submitting to the Mosaic covenant.

4. Paul reflects the various categories of Old Testament Law by his use of the terms. τὸν νόμον (Law/Torah tårwøtV;) τῶν ἐντολῶν ("your" Commandments ÔKyRtOwVxI;mI) ἐν δόγμασιν (Ordinances). In Psalm 119, these words are oftentimes thought to be synonyms for the Law as a generality, but actually relate to various categories of laws found in the Torah. Paul, by using these terms, indicates Jews and Gentiles have access to God's full revelation contained in the Five Books.

5. Some interpreters understand this passage to mean that the unity comes about because Jews are no longer obligated to keep the Torah and this is what Paul has in mind as the removal of the enmity. These same commentators would usually understand the term to "make inoperative" to mean abolish, in that Paul is stating that God abolished any further Jewish obligation to the Torah. This would not fit in with

Paul's general teaching, as he calls the Law "good" in Romans 7 and suggests to Timothy a list of uses for the Old Testament Scriptures (see 2 Tim. 3:16). The apostle uses the term katargh/saß, but I do not believe he is suggesting that the Torah or the Law is abolished. Rather, the division, described as the "wall of partition" (dividing wall), which should not be viewed as a literal wall (such as in the Temple), was made inoperative by the cross. The exclusive right of Jewish people to the Torah has been lifted and God's revelation in the Torah is now fully available to the Gentiles. Jews who accept Yeshua are free to keep Torah or not to keep it, but this is not what is under consideration here. It is the Gentiles who are the subject of discussion as the ones who were "far off"—but now brought near. Those who were strangers to the covenants and promises of God to the Jewish people are now able to receive these blessings through their relationship to Jesus, and now share a new common bond with the Jewish people and Messianic Jews in particular.

6. Similar passages are found in First Corinthians 12:13 and Colossians 3:11.

7. Also Ephesians 2:12: *"…that at that time you were without Christ, being aliens from the commonwealth of Israel and strangers from the covenants of promise, having no hope and without God in the world."*

CHAPTER 4

The Hebrew Bible's Foundation for the One New Man

**Dr. Ray Gannon, Director of Messianic Jewish Studies,
The King's University**

God the Creator and the Missio Dei

In the beginning, God created, and jubilant celebration began as the morning stars sang in symphony and the angels shouted for joy (see Job 38:7). We can conjecture that this harmonious adulation reached a crescendo with the unveiling of the apex of God's creative expression—the original Adam. God's keen interest in this unique accomplishment is evident in the opening verses of Genesis as He declares His profound satisfaction with the new Man created in God's own likeness to reflect God's very image.

God is seen in Genesis to be all-powerful, wholly appreciative of true beauty, given to artistic detail, and manifestly happy with all His creation, including Man. In Man, however, God most clearly demonstrates His great passion and fundamental self-assigned task *(missio dei)*—His own full self-disclosure. His image is replicated and His character revealed, not only in the existence of man, but also in the interaction of God with His creation. God wants to make Himself known and fully reveal the broad panorama of His divine Person and attributes, and vividly demonstrate the depths and heights of His gracious, holy, and loving character. In concert with that, God desires the worshipful affection of the very capstone of His created order, the new Man, the newly created human being.

Those goals are focused in what the New Covenant (NT) calls the One New Man. History has been an ongoing record of mankind's resistance to God's passion for unity and harmony with His creation. It also witnesses to God's persistence in bringing a remedy to the fracturing and separation that has characterized the human condition since the Fall of Man in the Garden. The One New Man demonstrates the ideal of unity through the observable harmony of Jews and Gentiles who serve and worship God together, while disclosing in their often culturally distinct but shared spiritual life the character of God.

In the Hebrew Bible, God laid a foundation for the eventual revelation of God's *One New Man* project, which is openly displayed in the working out of the *missio dei*, later testified to in the New Covenant. The One New Man ideal, so exalted in Paul's writings in particular, may have been "under the radar" of the Jewish national leaders, the Levitical priestly establishment, and the cultural engineers in ancient Israel. This was a mysterious biblical teaching not fully understood by the people of Israel. In some ways it was "manifestly invisible" as were the Messianic prophecies associated with the nature of Yeshua's first coming. The budding flower would only fully open with God's revelation in Yeshua. But there certainly is strong support in the Torah, the Prophets and the writings of the Hebrew Scriptures for God's revealed intention of both global redemption and His receiving great glory from every nation.

While biblical Israel may have found the divine One New Man project inconceivable in light of Israel's duties to be untainted by the contaminating sinful peoples around them, Israel's duties to the nations are rehearsed repeatedly in Hebrew Holy Writ. With sincere monotheistic Gentiles formally converting to Israelite religion throughout the biblical period, the Jewish expectation remained strong that Gentile believers would convert to Jewish religion and become a committed part of the Chosen Jewish people. That people could come into covenant relationship with God apart from total identification with the Torah society of Israel was beyond Jewish imagination.

Yet within the frame of the Hebrew Bible, it is clear God wanted grand diversity among His worshipers and had no intention of making the whole world Jewish. His interest was to make all nations and peoples very much like Himself so as to offer tribute to His own majestic glory. The seed of this intention, scattered throughout the Hebrew Bible, will come to rich harvest in the One New Man who fully exhibits the grandness of God while demonstrating His holy character.

God Created Man as a Reflection of Himself

Man (Hebrew, *Adam*) is the ultimate act or capstone of God's creation account. Into Man, God breathed His own *Ruach* (His very own breath, wind, spirit). Consistent with the *missio dei,* God's resolve to manifest His majestic glory to all creation, God conscientiously fashioned Man to reveal God's likeness.

Woman (Eve, *Chavah*) provided a loving balance to Man so that the two-part man-woman might together more perfectly display the genuine unity of God. The two became *basar echad* (one flesh) to demonstrate the Creator's internal harmony within the Godhead.

As exquisite as Adam was, and as profound a witness to God's unity as man and woman were together, one man-woman team could not adequately attest to the full richness of God's Person. Therefore, God created man and woman with the capacity to generate multitudes of additional men and women to create a world of peoples and nations that together could corporately offer a far grander mosaic tribute to the Majesty on High.

God's glorious creation of Man as mirror-reflection of God was vested with authority to govern his world with full accountability to his Maker. The Creator was happy to fellowship with Man in the cool of the day to enjoy the pristine truthfulness of Man's adoring spiritual worship.

Beyond comprehension is the divine agony God encountered with Man's rebellion. The progenitors of the human race defied the very purpose for Man's creation: That is, to accurately mirror the majestic glory and holiness of God. This now broken and shattered mirror offered only a distorted and perverted reflection of God.

A disappointed God may well have accepted Adam and Eve's annihilation if Man was but a failed experiment. But the God desiring grand seasons of spiritual intimacy with an adoring and worshipful mankind would initiate a plan of redemption and reconciliation. Man as the sanctified mirror image of God would be one day fully restored and the harmonious song of a worshipping humanity, accompanied by a grand variety of redeemed symphonic-orchestrated multi-cultural instruments, would be divinely retuned. Once again would God be able to say of His re-creation, *Tov meod!, "Very Good!"*

Chesed: God's Loving-kindnesses from Noah to the Patriarchs

When the multiplied generations of Adam's descendents fully abandoned God in their impiety and preference for idols to the

Creator, God's universal judgment ultimately fell upon Noah's entire generation. But Noah's progeny soon repeated the cosmic tendency to dismiss the claims of God upon a humankind deliberately formed for the express purpose of exhibiting the holy and righteous character of God. The repeated universal assault on God's sovereignty and Lordship could well have resulted in another global divine judgment upon sinful Man. But the Redeemer had a righteous strategy for the redemption of Man that began to surface in Genesis. This redemption would need to include a reassembling of the shattered mirror image of God into a fully restored and useful reflection of God's unity and majestic glory.

Genesis 10 provides a graphic of an earth filled with nations of peoples alienated from God that plainly demonstrates that God's eye was upon all the peoples and nations with their varied ethnic and cultural distinctions. These diversities of cultural expression met with God's approval, since greater cultural diversity potentially facilitated grander tribute to the multifaceted character of God.

God's vastness and amplified holiness required much more than a mere one-flesh Adam-and-Eve-team to fully exhibit His majesty. The searching out of the unfathomable depths and heights of God's beauty and character demanded the worshipful contribution of billions of males and females, multitudes from every family line and social strata, the totality of all ethnic and cultural groups, for all the generations of every nation and race to *begin* to orchestrate a symphony of universal praise worthy of the manifest glories of God.

The self-revealing God wants and needs a grand variety in human beings who express His glory through the agencies of a host of cultural styles or national forms with each one signally contributing something uniquely valuable to the manifestation of His glory that every other one fails to contribute. Each person and people group has been created to offer distinct tribute to yet another dimension of God's greatness.

The Tower of Babel event (see Gen. 11) immediately follows the divine issue of demographics (see Gen. 10). In light of God's desire for variety, it is clear why the human race is here radically diversified by direct divine action. The old and original human sin problem—the "lust for power," is manifested and powerfully accented at Babel. The widespread tendency to impose an individual preference or group cultural ideal for all human beings and the correspondent amassing of human energies to accomplish such agendas of natural men are here witnessed. Exploitive leadership at Babel sought to culturally shackle humankind, God's own chosen instrument of self-revelation. They wanted to control, to dominate, to "clone" an imposed likeness of themselves upon the very creation God wanted to use as a witness to His *own* likeness. They wanted to usurp God's position, creating God in man's image.

It was not their unity at Babel but their pursuit of uniformity that reeked before God. In hot pursuit of their own idealistic dreams and convictions of what "man" should be, they were oblivious to the Creator's desires for humankind. Since the collective at Babel was cemented together in opposition to God's diversity program, God resolved to shatter that monolithic structure and retake each people group one pebble at a time. The scattered remnants of humanity have essentially been at perpetual odds ever since. We can recover unity only in submission to the redeeming Creator in cooperation with His grand design.

The dispersion at Babel did not lessen the intensity of God's claims upon the tongues, minds, and actions of all humankind. He still demanded obedience to His revelation from all peoples. Any perpetuated human resistance to God would continue to result in national pain, social anguish, and international turmoil.

Israel: God's Mission Agency

In spite of this universe-wide unrequited love, God sustained His own loving campaign of full self-disclosure, His *missio dei*. The Lord pursued the full revelation of himself to Noah's progeny as He still longed for the day all people would become worshippers of their Creator God. The next step in the divine program for global manifestation of His glory came with the call of Abraham in Genesis 12:1-3. The Chosen People issuing from the loins of Abraham, Isaac, and Jacob were assigned the task of manifesting God to all nations. God promised Abraham that in his seed *"all the families of the earth will be blessed"* (Gen. 12:3 NASB). Abraham's becoming *"great and mighty nation"* will bless *"all the nations of the earth"* (Gen. 18:18 NASB).

The same genre of blessing is promised to Isaac:

And I will multiply your descendants as the stars of heaven, will give your descendants all these lands; and by your descendants all the nations of the earth shall be blessed (Genesis 26:4 NASB).

It was also promised to Jacob:

Your descendants will also be like the dust of the earth, and you will spread out to the west and to the east and to the north and to the south; and in you and in your descendants shall all the families of the earth be blessed (Genesis 28:14 NASB).

After the Exodus redemption experience and just prior to receiving the Ten Commandments in Exodus 20, Israel is instructed at the foot of Sinai that the newly liberated Hebrew slaves are divinely assigned be a *"kingdom of priests and a holy nation"* (Exod. 19:5-6 NASB). Israel is to function as a nation of worshipful intercessors, mirrors of God's holiness, reflectors of His light, teachers of His truth, and keepers of His testimonies.

The Jewish people are selected to be the refocused manifestation of God through His actions with Israel.

God seems to "lock on" to Israel as they represent His steadfast hope for the working out of His purposes. His *missio dei* then becomes inseparably tied together with this nation of ambassadors. If they should prove to be a disappointment to God, He will chasten, correct, and redeem them in order to expressly use them in the end for the divine objective of self-revelation as well as His cosmic mission agency of reconciliation of the nations to God.

Israel, in one sense, is to be countercultural. Operating in the spirit of prophecy, Israel is to offer all God's earthly nations prophetic challenge. Confronting iniquity and condemning all that is contrary to God's character, Israel is to be calling all peoples everywhere to repentance and reconciliation with God.

God chose (Hebrew: *bachar;* elected, selected) Israel—before one Jewish person existed—to be that particular or special people God would use to impact the nations. The Jewish people were to be God's instrument of revelation to all humankind as peoples and nations were alienated from the Creator and darkened in their understanding. It is plain to see that *God chose the Jews because He loved the Gentiles.* Israel was chosen to perform a task, engage in divine service, and execute a mission. Israel was set in contradistinction to idolatrous nations to serve God, reveal His glory, and to evangelically declare His mastery of the universe. The purpose of Israel's election or Chosen People status directly relates to the salvation of the Gentiles.

Israel is to function as God's prophetic channel of communication to the world, serving as a national apostolic team to the universe of men and women. Ministering as both priests and prophets, Israel is God's original agency of world missions.

The Means of Israel's Priestly and Prophetic Witness

Knowledge of the Passover deliverance from Egypt would be instructive to Israel and the nations for all time as it demonstrates God's capacity to deliver peoples and nations from oppression and bondage. The God of Israel was manifestly a Redeemer. God fashioned a covenant (Hebrew, *B'rit*) with Moses and Israel similar to the international treaties of ancient Mesopotamia. But in God's Mosaic Covenant with Israel, initiated by Israel's national birth resulting from the Passover exodus, God issues Israel an enlightened constitution and bylaws for national life.

Within the hand-crafted parchment of the *Torah* (Law) scroll, God instructs His children how to fashion life with additional codes for hygiene and healthy cuisine, agricultural guidelines for soil conservation, instructions for commerce and fair trade practices, social mores to foster peaceful communal living and a sense of patriotism, and so forth. God also made clear His purposes for Israel and Israel's mission.

As early as the story of Noah, there is clear recognition that God is committed to all life on earth and that all creation is directly accountable to God. God is likewise committed to the total elimination of human rebellion against God. The sinful state of humanity has prevented the fulfillment of God's own purposes for humankind and fostered the continued frustration of people everywhere.

Six times in Genesis God repeats that Israel is His vehicle for blessing all the peoples of the earth. Such regular repetition in Genesis alone was to clarify for Israel her God-issued destiny that was to then inform Israel's worldview. Israel was not to imagine herself as nationally superior as a result of being chosen. Rather, Israel was to be aware of her obligation to fulfill her mission (see Deut. 7:7-11). God is the owner and ruler of all nations and peoples (see Deut. 10:14-22; Exod. 19:4-6). Israel's election did not imply the rejection of other nations but, rather, God's resolve to redeem all peoples. The biblical message is that what God first accomplished in redeeming Israel, He is prepared to do for all nations.

Israel, as a kingdom of priests, is to offer Torah enlightenment to all comers. This would require Israel's own Torah knowledge and faithful Torah compliance for Israel's light to be seen (see Lev. 10:11; Deut. 33:10; Mal. 2:6-7). The prophets will later indict Israel as having submerged themselves in the very sins God wanted to prevent in the pagans (see Hos. 4:1-9). The pattern of Levitical priestly sacrifice would instruct the Gentiles in God's offense at sin and the necessity for perpetual sacrifice to atone (see Lev. 1-7).

God's constant presence (*Shechinah*) was to be an important realization to other peoples who found their deities so arbitrary, absent-minded, and distant. God's very presence with His chosen people verified Israel's distinctiveness and demonstrated what God was ready to do even for oppressed slave nations (see Exod. 29:44-46; 33:16). However, God's presence mandated ethical holiness and ritual cleanness (see Lev. 19:2; Deut. 4:6-8). Without atonement, holiness and cleanliness, God would not cohabit with Israel, thereby making Israel's distinctive quite blurred and dysfunctional.

The nations would come to understand the revelation of God by virtue of His presence, the restoration of His *Shechinah* to a fully repentant, faithfully obedient and spiritually clean Israel (see Ezek. 37:26-28). The result of a Spirit-filled nation of Israel in pursuit of her mission to the nations is Israel's successful priestly service for all nations see (see Isa. 60:1-3,19-20; Rev. 21:22-24). Israel's accomplishment of her destined mission is possible only when God's presence is no longer in *Galut* (exile) but is restored to Israel (see Zech. 8:3,7-8,20-23).

Due to Israel's lack of faithfulness to God's revelation in Torah, the Hebrew prophets express their utter horror at the mandatory divine chastening of an unbelieving and disobedient

Chosen People. Israel had culturally absorbed the darkness of pagan sinful patterns. Israel had grown to rely on alien nations and regional deities for her own sustenance.

Such behavior defiled the very people God wanted to use as models of holiness, as internationally engaged priests, and as anointed (Messianic) spokesmen for God to bring about the redemption of all nations from their spiritual oppression and to reconciliation with God. But even the adversarial nations that previously may have been used of God to administer divine chastening upon a light-defying Israel are called upon to subsequently praise the Lord and rejoice with Israel (see Deut. 32:27-43), thereby demonstrating God's collective destiny for all.

Hebrew Bible Mission Theology Found in the Psalms

Even with these frequent divine disappointments the Israelite judges and Hebrew prophets adamantly register with Israel and Judah, there was no compromise on God's resolve to use Israel as His Chosen People for His *missio dei,* His self-revelation to all peoples. The Psalms reflect an awareness of Israel's divinely issued spiritual responsibility to the nations. Even Psalm 2 reiterates four major apostolic themes: All nations are in rebellion against the Lord (verse 3); God is Sovereign (verses 4-6); God's Chosen People have a divine mission to the nations (verses 7-9); there is great hope for the nations and ethnic peoples of the earth as the call to repentance is extended to them (verses 10-12). These themes are rehearsed throughout the Psalms.

Plainly the psalmist believed that God is at work among the nations, bringing their agendas to naught. Their responsibility, like Israel's, is to follow the counsel of God and find divine blessings (see Ps. 33:10-12). All the *goyim* (nations) are called upon to acknowledge God and offer Him worship in God's Temple (see Ps. 68:31-32; 72:11,17,19). Israel is to call on all the families of the world to ascribe glory and strength to the Lord (see Ps. 96:3,7,10,13).

All peoples are summoned to laud God's praises, the judge of all nations (see Ps. 98:2-4,9). The nations are to worship the Lord, the God so identified with Israel (see Ps. 117:1-2). The godly spokesmen of prophetic Israel are to make known to all the sons of men God's mighty acts and His kingdom's eternal majestic glory; He is near all who call upon Him in truth and will keep all those who love Him (see Ps. 145:12-13,18,20). Nature itself declares the glorious works of God to the very end of the world (see Ps. 19:1-4). The idolatrous nations are to abandon their false deities and turn to the Lord (see Ps. 135:15-18), for all nations belong to God (see Ps. 47:7-9).

All the nations are in rebellion against the Lord (see Ps. 2:3); the unbelieving are caught up in false religion. But resistance against God is ultimately futile for all nations (see Ps. 33:13-17). All humankind should turn to God for salvation for He is near to help and is just and kind (see Ps. 145:15-20). Men and women to the ends of the earth are to fear and worship Israel's God (see Ps. 66; 67:6-7) even as Israel petitions the Creator for the Gentiles' salvation (see Ps. 67:3-5). The Psalms resound with confidence that the day is coming when all the families of the earth will universally worship God, their Creator (see Ps. 22:27; 86:9). Israel is to prophesy and declare to the nations God's mighty acts and the glories of His Kingdom's majestic splendor (see Ps. 145:12-13). This seems both to look back to Genesis 12:2-3 and anticipate the Messianic Mandate of Matthew 28:18-20.

Hebrew Bible Mission Theology Found in the Prophets

The Hebrew prophets served in two chief ways. First, they demonstrated how far afield Israel and Judah had gone from their divinely issued mandate. They pointed out the irony that the nation that was to reflect the light of God's holiness to all other nations had, in fact, taken upon itself the darkness of the nations around her. Second, the Hebrew prophets reiterated the divine resolve to use this same Chosen People for His original intention and objectives for Israel under the banner of Messiah.

The prophets were indignant that Israel and Judah had subverted God's intended program by their misconduct and defiance of God's revealed Word. For example, Israel had sustained the golden calf worship of their forefathers by fabricating gods with evil agendas designed only to accommodate their fabricators (see 1 Kings 12:28; 2 Kings 10:29). Rather than functioning as the chosen destroyers of humanly invented deities and sinful social agendas, Israel had become a pagan fellow participant. Israel's light had become darkness.

Regrettably, Israelite and Jewish religion offered a high-sounding belief system fully inconsistent with actual Jewish practices and lifestyles. The prophets protested that contemporary Jewish religion was devoid of the true righteousness so vital to Israel's mission (see Amos 2:6; 5:21-24; Mic. 3:1-3). Exploitation of the poor to enrich the few and obtaining exorbitant real estate holdings at the expense of the impoverished flew in the face of the Torah's call for social equity and justice. Thus, Israel's mission as the chosen model of holiness, righteousness, and social justice was firmly rejected by those chosen as God's prototype (see Ezek. 5:5-6).

The blending of God's pure ways with pagan darkness prevented the current generations from fulfilling their mandated destiny of successfully serving as chosen agents of the revelation of God to all peoples. Interactive dialogue with the pagans had led to compromise, and the blending of two opposing religious systems. The Israelites did not profess to reject God but added pagan features to their standard religious worship.

While relativistic paganism might be able to tolerate syncretism—that is, the combining of contrary beliefs and practices, biblical faith really cannot. The prophets proclaimed a pending punishment as a means to revitalizing Israel's pure faith, proper practice, and permanent mission.

With all the contemporary sin issues and warnings of pending judgments, the Hebrew prophets insisted that a chastened and corrected Israel would be restored to a place of divine usefulness for the *missio dei*. Israel's mission would yet be successfully accomplished. The Jewish people would be redeemed yet again, but this time by the Messiah's revelation and salvation-issuing accomplishments. Israel would then find herself embracing her commission to bless the nations (see Gen. 12:2-3; Exod. 19:5-6) and celebrating the missions theology of the Psalms. But for this to eventuate in ultimate success, King-Messiah himself must be at the helm of Israel and lead the Chosen People into the final victory of their God-determined task.

The Messiah, King of Israel, as the Catalytic Agent

The Son of David (see Matt. 1:1), the King of "All Israel," would discharge His universal role based on the earlier pattern established by the reign of King David. The prophets now clearly anticipated a Messianic Age in which the Messiah served as the catalyst enabling Israel to fulfill her destiny. In full partnership and identification with Yeshua, the redeemed Chosen People are addressed by God, *"You are my servant, Israel, in whom I will display my splendor"* (Isa. 49:3 NIV).

In the Book of Isaiah, it is clear that the Messiah Yeshua, God's appointed Anointed One, brings justice to the nations (see Isa. 42:1). He is appointed as God's Covenant with Israel (see Jer. 31:31-34; Matt. 26:26-28) and as a Light to the Nations, the One opening the eyes of the blind and liberating the imprisoned (see Isa. 42:6-7). He brings a new song, the song of salvation, to the ends of the earth. To Him, every knee will bow and every tongue swear allegiance (see Isa. 42:10; 45:22-23).

Messiah, God's catalytic Servant, will not only raise up the tribes of Jacob and restore Israel but will be the Light of the nations. Through Him salvation will extend to the ends of the planet (see Isa. 49:6). All flesh will honor the Lord as Savior and Redeemer (see Isa. 49:26). Messiah will be the means to establishing enlightened justice for all peoples (see Isa. 51:4-5). As the arm of the Lord, He will be seen in all nations and bring salvation to the ends of the earth (see Isa. 52:10). The previously ignorant Gentiles will see and understand (see Isa. 52:10,15).

It appears that the four Messianic "Suffering Servant" passages extending from Isaiah 40 to 53 have application (1) to Israel as the Chosen apostolic community, (2) to Yeshua who is the very embodiment and catalyst of global redemption, and (3) to the balance of true believers the world over. The Servant here (see Isa. 53) is undoubtedly both the Messiah Yeshua and His Chosen People Israel as well as the later non-Jewish members of the community of God who have all been sent into the world of nations for the common purpose of global redemption as the messengers of the Lord's prophetic testimony. Israel's mission cannot be accomplished without the agency of the Israel-recognized and God-honored Messianic leadership. The Messiah will lead the effort to carry the mandate to the ends of the earth (see Isa. 49:6) and will not stop until the mission is completed and righteousness reigns worldwide.

Jonah as Arch-typical Hebrew Prophetic Voice to the Non-Jewish World

Without elaborating long on Jonah, dimensions of his mission are consistent with the mission portrayed in the entire Hebrew Bible. Jonah was a common Jewish man with a prophetic calling to preach repentance to those outside the Israelite fold, the Ninevites of Assyria. Jonah had typical human fears as he had heard the tales of Assyrian cruelties. He dreaded personal encounter with an idolatrous, depraved society that was a recognized threat to Israel.

God is seen in Jonah as committed to showing lovingkindness to the nations in spite of the fears, prejudices, and frailties of His selected spokesmen. The Ninevites seem to respond in faith and obedience more readily than Jonah, God's handcrafted servant. That they are spared demonstrates that God is concerned about the well-being and redemption of all peoples. Jonah is also a clear demonstration of how Israel could be a light to the Gentiles and a blessing to the nations long before the first appearance of Messiah.

Biblically, entire populations can be the legitimate target of mission enterprise. Whole families, complete neighborhoods, entire cities, and yes, even nations can be spiritually redeemed. The key to evangelistic success is faith and obedience. If the Book of Jonah is called the "fish story" of the Bible, perhaps that label should apply more to Jonah trying to wiggle off the prophetic hook than referencing a whale. Excuses won't do the Kingdom of God any good. Believers are the voices God needs to prophesy to the nations. The One New Man of the New Covenant denotes a call of God to each individual, Jew or Gentile, to fulfill this mission.

The Jewish Mission during the Intertestamental Period

The *synagogue* as an institution was developed in Babylon during the Babylonian captivity after 586 B.C. The synagogue developed a liturgical service corresponding to that of the destroyed Temple and organized to preserve Jewish faith by prayer, study, and social cohesiveness, and to offer an apologetic for Jewish perpetuity. The synagogue *(Beth Knesset)* was open to everyone in Diaspora, the Jewish exile. Its oral character, strict monotheism, and regimented religious lifestyle would have great magnetism for disenfranchised pagans, so disillusioned by the chaos brought on by idolatrous immorality.

When 50,000 Jews returned with Zerubbabel to Zion, the synagogue as an institution was carried back to the Promised Land. Over the course of time, half of the Jewish world was living in dispersion. Distant as they were from the land of Israel and from the Temple, they found the synagogue model for sustaining Jewish life by means of Torah study, regular prayer, and social accountability to be highly useful to Jewish communities everywhere.

Apocalyptic literature helped to spur on missionary activity in the Intertestamental period (approximately 400 B.C. to 70 A.D.). Jewish religion was in the process of going through a great metamorphosis from a strictly Torah-based, temple-priesthood functioning, land-centered religion to an increasingly rabbinic Synagogue-centered and Diaspora-friendly faith. About 4.5 million Jewish people represented 7 percent of the total population of the Roman Empire. Three million of these were based in the Middle East, while 1.5 million resided in Asia Minor (modern Turkey), Europe, and across Northern Africa.

Jewish religion in Diaspora became highly proselytizing and made serious efforts at converting pagans to Jewish religion. New ideas of the Jewish mission, the last days, the messianic age, and new emphases on the one universal God and His commitment to the emancipation of the pagans from idolatrous and immoral practices, all combined to strongly motivate Diaspora Jews to communicate their monotheism to the curious around them. Thus, a rapidly changing Jewish religion demonstrated great zeal for proselytizing Gentiles.

Knowledge that the universal God would judge all the nations and conviction that the Kingdom of God was really for the righteous of all peoples compelled many in Israel to recognize the high and holy calling God had issued Israel—that is, they were to minister spiritual things to other peoples and nations. Jews were becoming more eager to invite pagans to seriously consider the claims of God as revealed in Scripture. Some even anticipated that Jewish religion was destined to become a universal faith. This made thousands of Diaspora Jews religiously tolerant and even hopeful for the conversion of myriads of Gentile God-fearers.

Modern scholars conclude, in fact, that perhaps hundreds of thousands of Jews throughout the Diaspora were Gentile converts. Paul's description of Jewish enthusiasm for offering spiritual counsel to the Gentiles in Romans 2:19-20 would lend itself in support of this opinion. Many Gentiles involved in the mystery religions of the era considered Jewish religion superior. Monotheism and Bible-based morality had strong attraction to those seeking moral transformation. So effective were Jewish missionaries that Egyptian philosophers were among those who angrily protested "excessive" Jewish influence on non-Jews.

The general openness toward travelers and Gentiles in the Jewish synagogue context laid the foundation for later apostolic activities among both Jews and Gentiles. The synagogue environment created a vast host of Gentile God-fearers whom Paul discovered were ready to respond to the Gospel. In a real sense, the apostolic mission done in obedience to the Messianic Mandate to preach to Gentiles as observed in the Book of Acts was, in important part, a continuation or extension of the originally issued Jewish mission as contemporarily exercised in synagogue life (see Gen. 12:1-3; Exod. 19:5-6).

The Hebrew Bible Anticipates the Messianic Conquest of All Nations

The Hebrew Bible and the Intertestamental period then laid the foundation for the universal proclamation of the Gospel called for by the Messiah Yeshua at the conclusion of His earthly ministry. Nothing was suggested in the words of Yeshua's Messianic Mandate that was inconsistent with all that God had already given to Israel in the Hebrew Bible and progressively expounded throughout Jewish history.

Yeshua stood before the House of Israel and succinctly instructed them, perhaps with more particularity and straightforward assertion, but with an inclusive outreach emphasis fully consistent with all that God's Spirit had been communicating with Israel since patriarchal times. Indeed, this was the fulfillment of all that had gone before. If the mission of Israel had been seen through a glass darkly, the Perfect One now brought all the illumination necessary to the issue for those early Jewish believers to gain proper global focus.

The Great Commission or Messianic Mandate (see Matt. 28:18-20) is not given in a contemporary vacuum of understanding. Not only were Yeshua's disciples familiar with the biblical record, the patriarchal narratives, the Passover/Exodus redemption event, the Psalms and prophetic testimonies, and the mission trends of the Jewish world in the years prior to the coming of Yeshua, but His disciples had received private instruction and mentoring from the Master Agent of redemption himself.

The twelve remembered their experiences of being sent out to proclaim *"the Kingdom of God is at hand"* early in their time with Yeshua (see Matt. 10; Mark 6:7-13; Luke 9:1-16). They recalled His deploying the evangelistic energies of the seventy in Luke 10:1-24, and of course of Yeshua's sending of the "called-out ones" in John 20:21. Yeshua's teachings and ministry activities were modeled for the disciples that He might show them how God desired to use them.

Of course, it was the Great Commission (see Luke 24:44-49; Acts 1:8) that universalized the ministry of Yeshua. To that point, His ministry had been generally limited to the Jewish people. He stated that He was *"not sent but unto the lost sheep of the House of Israel"* (Matt. 15:24 KJV). It strikes many as strange that Yeshua responded as He did to the Syrophoenician woman (see Mark 7:27) and instructed His disciples to work with none other than Jews (see Matt. 10:5-6).

Why did Yeshua focus so keenly on the Chosen People? God's promises to the patriarchs, kings, and prophets were in focus. Israel was biblically to function as the prime sender or communicator of God's revelation. As a result of Jewish apostolic effectiveness among Gentile fruit, others would surely join in the *missio dei* over the course of time. But without "all Israel" keenly immersed in the task, the global assignment would not be successfully concluded.

The Great Commission had been taken seriously, but it did not radically change first-century Messianic Jewish self-understanding nor compel Yeshua's Jewish followers to immediate activity that varied much from what they had always known and believed. Israel, of course, was to be the agent for proclaiming the Kingdom of God universally. Now that the Messiah-ship of Yeshua was recognizable, believing Jews must preach the resurrected Yeshua as both Lord and Messiah.

Naturally, redemption in Yeshua was for all peoples since faith in Him was the sole means to salvation. But before Israel would be able to effectively preach the resurrected Messiah and proclaim genuine reconciliation to God universally, Israel must herself come to faith in Yeshua. This was the very reason Paul, the "apostle to the Gentiles," always preached "to the Jew first" and the balance of the apostles spent their lives primarily preaching to Jews.

The New Covenant (NT) mission task is uniquely focused and clearly assigned by the Messiah of Israel, Yeshua himself. But the NT mission issued to the first-century Jewish believers was fundamentally the same call to participation in global redemption that Israel had been chosen for since the time of Abraham. The NT Messianic Mandate is essentially the logical extension or perpetuation of the original Hebrew Bible mission. The essential difference is that now the Messiah Yeshua is the recognized source of energy for the mission's successful accomplishment. He is the catalyst who transforms Israel into that highly successful mission society God has always proclaimed Israel's destiny to be.

The NT, no more clearly than the Hebrew Bible, enunciated that the God of Israel is also the God of the nations. Yeshua himself is proclaimed the Lord of all cultures, language groups, ethnic stripes, and nations. The new birth experience is available to all who follow the Lord of God's people, who trust and obey Yeshua. Again, this is essentially the same mission task but now more explicitly expressed—that is, *"Disciple all nations"* (see Matt. 28.19).

It is in this same spirit of the "ministry of reconciliation" (see 2 Cor. 5:18) that the Jewish Messiah stands on Olivet and sends apostolic Israel to the far reaches of the world to proclaim reconciliation to God through the agency of Israel's Messiah. Peoples of every ethnic persuasion to the uttermost parts of the earth are to confess Yeshua as Lord and follow Him however and wherever He may lead.

Between the resurrection and the Second Coming, this team of Messianic Jews and grafted-on Gentiles are to be out preaching the Kingdom of God to the ends of the earth, to all places of human habitation, to all people groups. Only then will salvation history climax, come to its epitome, and reach its crescendo in God's praise.

Conclusion

To offer God the glory that is genuinely due His name requires every Jewish person, every Christian, every human being—the entire Jewish community and the whole Body of Christ, the full number of the more than half-billion Pentecostals and Charismatics in today's world, the entire global Christian community including all Evangelicals, Protestants, Catholics, and Orthodox, of all humanity's generations since Adam, *all combined*—to plumb the depths, to reach the heights, to travel the width and length of God's glory so as to only *start* the song of the fully scored harmonization of the eternal singing of His praises.

It is for this very truth and purpose that the apostle Paul so strongly condemned cultural imperialism in Galatians (e.g., the human tendency to mandate the adoption of the soul-winner's own cultural style or preference as authentication of the new believer's genuine salvation experience). This, in effect, stifles freedom of expression and curtails the very pursuit of righteously expressed variety that God really desires. Christians guilty of *cultural imperialism* often attempt to compel newer believers in Yeshua to function within the soul winner's own particular Christian cultural "comfort zone" and abandon the new believer's cultural distinctive. But such mimicking of the soul winner's own cultural baggage is counterproductive to God's purposes as it militates against the development of the divinely desired mosaic that brings the fuller revelation of God's majestic glory.

Since God's person and presence reside in Yeshua (see Col. 1:19; 2:9), the universality of Israel's mission to the nations can only be accomplished when Yeshua is the desired kingly presence within a repentant, submissive and faithfully obedient national Israel. In the interim, Yeshua is present among the redeemed of all nations and has effectively made the regenerated of all peoples fellow-heirs with Israel (see Col. 1:27; Eph. 3:6).

The current world of nations, so alienated from one another in their common defiance of God's authority, ultimately can find reconciliation and reunification even as they rejoice over the broken stones of the wall of partition long since demolished by Yeshua's own cross (see Eph. 2:14-16). Centering their identities around the accomplishments of the Messiah Yeshua, the reconciled and reunited remnants of culturally diversified humanity will fashion a grand new mosaic in successful tribute to God's glory.

Those redeemed by the blood of God's Lamb, the spiritually regenerate of all peoples, tongues, and nations, should testify to God in every imaginable way through every conceivable instrument. When all peoples and nations fully live like the Master, Yeshua, the *Second* Adam, only then will they have begun to properly give God the glory due His Holy Name.

Herein lies the culmination of the Hebrew Bible's hope for a redeemed humanity, with the Second Adam orchestrating the grand symphony of blood-bought worshippers, Jews and Gentiles, who are joined as One New Man. Israel and the nations will ever harmonize together while singing the song of the redeemed. But only with the public witness of the coming of the two camps into "One New Man" in Yeshua shall that grand international and intergenerational voice fully resound the majestic glories of God's praiseworthiness so that the song is universally and perpetually heard.

God's eternal faithfulness to His Chosen People, in spite of the protests of many in Israel for their centuries of persecution, cannot be denied in light of the modern restoration of national Israel in a manner so consistent with the proclamation and spirit of Hebrew prophecy. It is time for "all Israel" to acknowledge the One that God has made "The King of Israel," the appointed Anointed One to lead Israel into her biblically promised destiny.

Apostolic teaching makes it clear that God is wanting the Gentile fruit, still being harvested from the early labors of Messianic Jewish apostles, to enter into such fullness of anointing and spiritual service to Israel as to successfully provoke Israel to spiritual jealousy and faith in Yeshua. Only then can God's desires for Israel and the nations find satisfaction. Only then will He be able to look upon a humanity truly mirroring His image and say, *Tov Meod,* "Very Good!"

CHAPTER 5

Denominations, Messianic Jews, and the One New Man

Dr. Daniel C. Juster, Tikkun International, Director

Long before Yeshua directed his disciples to take the Gospel of the kingdom of God to the whole world, he had already established unity as a fundamental prerequisite for the success of their mission. It was His prayer for them, *"That they all may be one...that the world may believe that You sent Me"* (John 17:21). Scripture tells us that we are to reflect the reality of being the One New Man (see Eph. 2:15), joined in unity without the wall of partition. Unfortunately, history has been a story of separation more than it has unity.

The rise of denominations is generally presented as a manifestation of sin and division that challenges the unity of the One New Man and the fulfillment of the prayer of Yeshua. It is a sad chapter in Christian history that we are overcoming. Some assert that a return to Jewish roots is a key to a restoration of unity and the end of denominations.

There is some truth to this perception, but it is not in itself adequate. Much was lost as the Church distanced itself from its beginnings, but that is more of a symptom than the cause. Simply restoring a link to Jewish heritage, important as I believe that is, will not eliminate division. Likewise, denominationalism itself is a reflection of a deeper, fundamental problem.

It is true that our level of division today is unhealthy and detrimental. The existence of denominations, however, is not the real problem. Rather, it is competitiveness. I often say that we no longer just have major denominations, but an ideal of independence that in no way can be squared with a biblical understanding of our unity in Yeshua and the corporate reality of His Body. Independent congregations compete with other independent congregations in every major city in the West (and beyond), who practice a kind of competitive free-enterprise ecclesiology. Some level of competition is unavoidable since people will choose congregations that do a good job in what they are seeking. However, the heart of true leaders should be to embrace a love that desires the success of all fellow leaders and legitimate congregations!

If we are going to evaluate denominations and the way forward to the unity for which Yeshua prays, we do have to have a vision of the goal. That goal can only be understood from the New Covenant Scriptures and an understanding of the development of denominationalism. So we begin with a reflection of the biblical texts and an overview of the history of fragmentation within the Church.

The Jewish Context of the Early Church

In the first period of its existence, the post-Pentecost community of believers in Jerusalem manifested the ideal of the prayer of Yeshua, that they would be one. Acts 2:42-48 tells us that the community was in wonderful unity and that the believers had such a heart of love and sharing that they did not consider their own possessions as only for themselves, but sold property and gave to everyone in the community who had need.

The Church in Jerusalem constituted a very large community. Some believe that what began with 120 people in Acts 1 and exploded in a single day to 3,000 in Acts 2, had grown by Acts 21 to tens of thousands of believers, meeting from house to house. It was not possible for that many to meet regularly as one large congregation.

I believe this early Church provides us with a model of Yeshua's ideal for unity. First of all, they had a common faith. Note that the Church was primarily Jewish. There was an adherence to the Messianic traditions of Judaism, and the fulfillment of those traditions in Yeshua, that gave coherence and stability to all that the Church did. As I will contend, this fact does not mean that the Church needs to become Jewish. But it is impossible to fully understand and live the life of Yeshua without recognizing that he was Jewish, that his earthly ministry took place in the context of a Jewish culture, and most importantly, that He is the fulfillment of Jewish Scripture.

Second, the early church was radically committed to Yeshua, not to a denominational group. They were one in community. They met in many locales, in individual homes in small groups, yet they constituted One Body. Being in community meant care and concern for each other, which resulted in many selling property and assisting those who were in need. There was an overriding sense of their oneness. It was the Church of Yeshua that lived in the city of Jerusalem, regardless of the specific meeting place or personal associations. They were all in it together.

Third, a point of great importance, though often overlooked, they were united in accountability. Acts 2:42 tells us, *"They gave themselves to the apostles' teaching."* There was a unified deference to the appointed leaders. Though made up of thousands of people meeting in many places, they were governed by one eldership over the whole city. Yeshua chose 12 disciples and gave them authority. The 12 disciples became the eldership government for the entire city, later under the leadership of the apostle Jacob (James). This structure reflected the influences of the Jewish synagogue and the Sanhedrin, both of which were ruled by a council of elders.

At its inception, the Church was almost entirely Jewish in every way, in membership, in leadership, in belief, and in practice, and largely confined to Jerusalem. As the Jerusalem community was established, prophecy, signs, and wonders confirmed that it was not to remain so. Guided by the hand of God, the message of Yeshua rapidly spread to other cities of Israel, then outside the national boundaries.

The traveling apostles, as they carried the Gospel to other nations, and most notably Paul-Saul, established the same government that we find in Jerusalem. We read that Paul appointed elders. In addition, Titus was commanded to appoint elders. Elders were appointed in succession by other elders. They are not self-appointed or the product of an election where candidates ran against one another (see Acts 14:23; Titus 1:5). Apostles continued to have authority in the cities where they planted. This authority was alongside of that of the elders.

Yet, in spite of the rapid growth that, in just a few decades, covered a third of the known world, the basic elements that characterized the Jerusalem Church remained dominant features. The Jewish heritage is still seen even in such mundane areas as the basic order of service when believers met. Believers were still known for their love for each other.

The leaders of the Jerusalem community still had primacy with the whole of the movement. This was demonstrated by the fact that when there was a major dispute on the requirements for Gentiles in regard to circumcision, Jewish life and practice, leaders were able to convene the council of apostles and elders to render a decision that was binding on all the congregations or communities throughout the world (see Acts 15). Unity in government was maintained, as well as a link to the Church's past, without requiring Gentile believers to become Jewish.

I believe that this provides us with a model of what the Body of Believers should look like. It was Jewish rooted in understanding. There was One New Man of Jew and Gentile. Jews lived a Jewish life and Gentiles were free to not embrace Jewish life. In addition, there was a means of overarching decision making for the whole Body. The early Church was united in tradition and faith, in community and in government. When First Corinthians 1:10-17 tells us that division or schism is serious sin, it is because division undermines these essential characteristics.

The Election of Israel

As Christianity moved into its second century, the factors that made the early church a model of the One New Man came under attack, often without the participants in the debates realizing what was at stake. Ironically, the desire to protect the unity of the Church gradually, by small but significant steps, led to the destruction of that unity.

In the wake of the fall of Jerusalem and the destruction of the Temple in the first century, most Church leadership lost the apostolic view of the continued election of the ethnic Jewish people. The devastation during the battle over Jerusalem, including the loss of perhaps a million or more people, was so great that many of the Church fathers could no longer believe in the election of ethnic Israel. Disregarding the declaration of Romans 11:28-29 that, *"Though they are enemies of the Gospel...they are elect and beloved for the sake of the fathers,"* and that *"God's gifts and calling (to Israel) are irrevocable,"* the new Gentile leaders came to falsely believe that Israel's election was now transferred to the new and true spiritual Israel, the Church.

This belief that the Church had replaced Israel, known today as replacement theology or supersessionism, did not eliminate the influence of the Jewish model. Indeed, thinking of herself as a new Israel, the Church continued to embrace a great deal that was inherited from the Messianic Jews and the Jewish Apostles. Much in the forms of worship continued, including psalms, singing of the Holy, Holy, Holy (*Sanctus*) which is the *Kedusha*, faith in One God and the Messiah, Scripture reading, benedictions, the meaning of communion in the sacrifice of Yeshua as a fulfillment of the meaning of Temple sacrifices, Passover and Yom Kippur symbolism and benedictions. In addition, as the Church developed architecture, the altar and table of showbread were replicated in the church altar. The seven-branched lampstand and the eternal light were reproduced as well. Jewish roots of expression have never been lost from the Church, just unrecognized and sometimes disguised and unappreciated.

In spite of the continued influence of the Church's Jewish heritage, the loss of belief in the election of ethnic Israel planted the seed that would gradually lead to a loss of many important elements of Messianic belief. This later created divisions over doctrinal debates that need never have happened. Some of these will be noted in the following pages.

Unity, Catholic and Orthodox

Some church historians say that even by the end of the first century, many of the churches throughout Asia were composed of thousands of believers meeting in house congregations. The rapid growth and the necessity of maintaining a multiplicity of gathering places did not produce a sense of isolation or competition between those groups. They still belonged to the Church of whatever city they lived in. The church of Ephesus, for example, encompassed all believers in the city of Ephesus, regardless of which home meeting they frequented.

We should entertain the idea that this sense of community reflects the fact that the second-century Church preserved governmental structures that are rooted in apostolic foundations. Elders were appointed in every city where the Church was planted. The letters of the Church fathers of the second century indicate the continuance of this model for church government. There was an eldership in each city over all the gatherings. In addition, there was a first among equals among the elders, called a bishop.

This raises several questions. Many New Testament scholars believe that the terms "elder" and "bishop" were equivalents in the New Testament. First Timothy 3 and Titus 1 give the same instructions for church leaders, the prior calling them elders and the latter bishops or overseers. These passages, along with Acts, show a plurality of elders. Of significance to our understanding of Church government, elders were not self-appointed, but were appointed and ordained by other elders and perhaps apostles. There was a succession, parallel to early Rabbinic Judaism, in which rabbis were appointed by other rabbis.

This was the basic organization of the Church as it moved through the second century. The death of the last of the original Apostles, however, brought many new challenges. Some charismatic leaders departed from the teaching of the Apostles, in some cases, gaining significant followings. Most prominent, and most dangerous, were teachers who supported Gnostic heresies, teachings that denied the incarnation, or made salvation a matter of a progress of knowledge disciplines.

J.N.D. Kelly well argued that the response of the churches was to increase the role of the bishop and to establish submission to the bishop as a safeguard of apostolic practice.[1] Some see a transition from a plurality of elders government to a monarchial bishop. The early second-century Church father Ignatius, bishop of Antioch, asserted the role of the bishops as successors to the Apostles. This doctrine of apostolic succession came very early.

Concern for the unity of the Church in doctrine and practice was paramount. At this early stage, believers were already moving toward defining themselves not in their relationship to Yeshua and to each other, but in their adherence to doctrine. Community, the concern and love for one another, began to give way to concern for organization and form. The preservation of apostolic government served as a safeguard against heresy and schism, but those concerns resulted in a change of governmental structure, with power becoming increasingly consolidated in fewer elders and bishops.

In spite of the attempts to preserve unity, there were intense battles by the end of the second century. Many today would be considered trivial matters, but they created great dissension in the Church at that time.

For example, the eastern and western churches vigorously disagreed about when to celebrate the death and resurrection of Yeshua. The western church followed a solar calendar, which they claimed to be based in apostolic tradition. Polycrates, bishop of Antioch, also claimed apostolic tradition for his lunar calendar, and the celebration of both the death and resurrection of Yeshua on the Jewish date of Passover, 14-15 Nisan. Oscar Sakarsune, a Lutheran historian-theologian and friend of the Messianic Jewish movement, argues that the different traditions reflected the different calendars in the first century Jewish community, and the different choices made for celebration in the East and the West.[2]

Victor, bishop of Rome, threatened to excommunicate those who disagreed with him. He claimed that as bishop of Rome, he had higher authority than Antioch. First of all, Rome was the capital of the empire. It was natural for Victor to see the Roman bishop as the superior bishop. There was no longer a Jewish bishop in Jerusalem. Second, the strong tradition that both Peter and Paul exercised authority in Rome and were executed there gave a sense of the primacy of Rome.

We see in this disagreement a distinct movement toward denominationalism. It was a key factor in the eventual split between east and west. Yet, in spite of the division of opinion, there was still one institutional Church in the world, and this would continue for 850 years. This should cause those from more independent orientations to pause and consider their presuppositions. No matter how intense the debate and disagreement, the Church as a whole was permeated with the understanding that unity was essential. The Church was thought of in terms of all believers living anywhere on the earth. The universal Church was divided only by geographical considerations and the impossibility of the many thousands in each major city meeting in a single location. Each city contained one Church that met in many smaller groups. Rarely was anyone willing to take the route of independence.

The seeds of denominationalism had been sown, however. Other deep and intense battles contributed further to the move in that direction. Arius inspired a movement of bishops that influenced the Church to almost abandon the orthodox view of the deity and humanity of Yeshua.

The first Council of Nicea in 325 called together a council of bishops to settle the issue. For Constantine, Roman emperor at that time, Christianity could be a force for unity in the Roman Empire, but only if it was itself unified. Under his prodding, the bishops agreed to clear statements on the deity and humanity of Jesus, the Tri-unity of God and the dating for the celebration of the resurrection.

Some Messianic Jews invalidate the Council, especially in light of the anti-Semitic letter of Constantine. It is claimed that there were no Messianic Jewish bishops included. Moreover, the replacement of Israel with the Church was sufficiently established that we do not know of Jewish bishops living a Jewish life during that time.

That doesn't mean that the Jewish influence was gone. Skarsaune argues that the basic statement of the Nicean confession was lifted from Scriptural passages and preserved a Jewish New Testament faith against the Hellenizing influence of Arius. Indeed, the Council was much better than we would have expected in the light of the rejection of Jewish input. For a season, both east and west would celebrate the resurrection on the same date. However, this victory was temporary. New calendar calculations would eventually cause a split between East and West.

Constantine's efforts to maintain unity set a trajectory that would lead to the embrace of Christianity as the state religion of the Roman Empire some 50 years later. On the surface it appeared to be a victory for the Church. But there were inherent problems in this victory. To maintain the outward appearance of unity, the fabric of true unity had been seriously damaged. The Church had lost much of its connection to its Jewish roots and traditions. The sense of community that characterized the early church largely was obscured by the consolidation of governing power in the hands of a single bishop. Subservience to the organization replaced submission to the community of believers.

Christianity gave the world the idea of a universal faith that transcended ethnic and state governments. Making Christianity the state religion would compromise the independence of church government and state government. It would take 1,300 years before the first separation of church and state.

Judaism, of course, was the religion of Israel, and also predicted the universal acceptance of the God of Israel. Yet this vision of the Jewish prophets included the Messiah's rule of all national or ethnic governments as well. Until the government of

Messiah became reality, separation was very important. Separation allowed the government of the Church to remain in the hands of spiritual leaders, who were charged with the shepherding of the people. In contrast, under the control of the state, spiritual values were subverted to meet political goals.

Separation for Purity

It should be noted that the movement toward denominationalism grew out of many legitimate concerns for the preservation of Church life and unity. The consolidation of authority in the hands of a single bishop was a response to the infiltration of heretical teaching. It was believed that the tighter control of a single leader would empower him to deal more effectively with dissidents, eliminating the effects of schism.

This was exemplified by a threat to the unity of the Church that appeared in the fourth and fifth century, known as the Donatist Movement. The Donatists reacted to corruption and sin in the Church. Their solution was to create a more pure church by separating themselves.

Augustine, prominent church leader at the beginning of the fifth century, considered the separation to be a greater threat to the Church than the corruption. He vigorously opposed the separation and delineated the standards for legitimate and illegitimate separation. Augustine said that separation is only legitimate when the Church officially embraces moral and doctrinal error of a foundationally important level or denies foundational truth. Leaders who are ordained but corrupt are still to be respected for the office and have to be removed by legitimate processes. Augustine knew that separating for purity would lead to fragmentation. Most large church bodies—Catholic, Protestant, and Eastern have followed his teaching on this.

By this time in Church history, most bishops rejected the legitimacy of Jewish life in Yeshua. They viewed Jewishness as deeply offensive to God and clearly against His will. The wall of hostility between Jew and Gentile was growing higher. Unity, as perceived in that day, did not include the One New Man of Ephesians.

Anti-Jewishness was not codified in a universal Church Council until Nicea II in A.D. 787. However, the separation of the Gentile Church from its Jewish roots had been moving toward outright rejection and exclusion for many centuries. Regional councils did make such the law of the churches for their regions, including Alvira, Spain in A.D. 306 to 307 and Antioch in 316. The tone of anti-Semitism in these decrees was quite stunning.

We can well wonder what Jewish roots of understanding would have meant in some of the controversies. The Church moved in directions that would never have been accepted by Messianic believers. For example, in the eighth century a terrible battle was fought over the place of images in worship. The iconoclasts were a strong force, but ultimately were defeated by the proponents of icons and statues, who argued that the incarnation implied a loosening of the commandment against image making found in the Ten Commandments. In addition, a continued elevation of Mary and the saints for intercession and worship was bound to cause future splits due to the fact that some would read Scripture as precluding such practices.

There were now churches in different regions that were not accepted as Orthodox. The Copts of Egypt, the Ethiopian Christians (who kept the Jewish Sabbath and circumcised their sons due to believing they were descendants of Jews), Armenians, and others were condemned as having a deficient Christology. This is too complex to explain here; however, these different regional-ethnic churches were not in communion with the mainstream Orthodox-Catholic Church. The Church as a whole had not fragmented, but increasingly, there were isolated elements.

Finally, the great split between East and West took place. The assertion of the primacy of Rome and its authority over all churches, issues of interpretation of the Trinity, and historical cultural developments led to a final split. The Eastern Orthodox Churches recognized the greater weight of Rome for honor, and also gave a greater weight to the most ancient bishoprics, but asserted the basic equality of all Patriarchs or leading bishops. At most, Rome could be the first among equals. Rome argued that the unity of the Church required an ultimate submission to the bishop of Rome and the centrality of being in continued communion with him.

So at the close of the eleventh century we find that the fractioning of the Church had become serious. We not only have the split in the East and West, but the split from the other ethnic churches already mentioned. The beginnings of denominationalism were in place. The character of the Church had changed radically from the early days, when it was known for its unity.

I do want to note that many great saints were doing great work in extending the Gospel to the nations and showing works of love that were most praiseworthy. The work of the Church did continue in many wonderful ways, and the gates of Hell did not prevail in spite of these difficulties.

The Vision of the Reformation

The Reformation was a Western Church phenomenon. The catalyst was the awesome corruption in the Roman Catholic Church. This included the sale of indulgences that were said to release souls from purgatory and the moral corruption of bishops and priests. This is not to say there were not godly people in the Roman Catholic Church. There were many, but the corruption reached an unprecedented level.

Doctrinal issues were also paramount. This included the publishing and posting of the doctrine of justification by faith by Martin Luther, in opposition to the widespread Catholic confusion on the relationship of faith and works. This position challenged issues such as the worship of Mary and the saints and the absolute authority of the popes and bishops for the interpretation of Scripture. The Reformers respected councils and leadership, but raised the Scriptures to authority above its interpreters.

It is important to say that the first reformers did not want to leave the Catholic Church but to reform it. Why? Because they had a great respect for the unity of the Church and a conviction about the sin of schism. They had to be forced out.

Luther's call for reformation was clearly a call for repentance, not a call for division and separation. When separation became necessary, it was very challenging. We have to remember that the power of the state enforced the hegemony of the Catholic Church. The support of state princes made the Reformation possible. Some supported Luther for pious reasons and some for reasons of power. When the split took place, Luther at least hoped that there would be one Reformation Church in distinction from the Catholic Church.

The Reformation under John Calvin also sought to establish the ideal of one Reformation Church. The government of Calvinism continued to follow the biblical model of an eldership of the city overseeing all the churches of the city.

We sadly note that the early Luther was very pro-Jewish, but the later Luther embraced anti-Semitism, with terrible consequences for Germany and the world. Replacement theology continued to be dominant in the Reformation churches. There was an exception, however; for some of the Puritans began to read the Hebrew text more straightforwardly and could not dismiss the promises to ethnic Israel, nor could they see these promises as merely fulfilled in the Church as the New and True Israel.

The Puritans had a "both and" idea of Israel—both the Church as spiritual Israel and ethnic Israel as still important and elect. This prepared the way for a very pro-Jewish orientation in both England and America. A minority actually believed in the literal fulfillment of the promises to Israel in the Land. In addition, the Puritans influenced Lutheran Pietism, first in Germany and then in Scandinavia, whose leaders developed a very deep commitment to the Jewish people and a belief in their continued election and restoration. Romans 9-11, interpreted as a reaffirmation of a key role for ethnic Israel, was very important in some streams of Puritanism and Lutheran Pietism.

While replacement theology still dominated, I believe that the Reformers did return the Church in some ways to the original biblical Jewish orientation. Many of the elements that had led to fractioning of the Church were addressed. Reformers set out to make leadership more responsible. The elevation of Scripture was an attempt to return to a unity of faith.

Alas, the three key reformers could not agree on some of the key issues of doctrine. There were differences in church government positions. In addition, there was a fierce debate on the nature of Communion. The result of these and other disputes was a split Reformation.

Finally we note the Anabaptist Reformation, which embraced the separation of the church and the state, pacifism, and the adult baptism of believers. We know the Anabaptists today under the names Mennonite, Amish, and Church of the Brethren. Many died for their faith in bucking State churches, Catholic and Protestant. Toleration for Anabaptists would not be established for some years. Later edicts of toleration would allow for freedom of religion, however, the full separation of church and state would not be established until the American Colony of Rhode Island under Baptist Roger Williams. This was understood in terms of separating civil government from church government, but never as separating the state from responsibility to God and his laws.

What is our assessment of the rise of denominationalism by this point in history? We note that state control and hatred for schism precluded greater fragmentation. The denominations in the beginning of the Reformation era generally reflected two important convictions. The first is the ideal that there should be one Church that follows the truth. In addition, there was no acceptance of the idea of independent local congregations. The linkage of congregations to denominations provided mutual accountability, the preservation of sound doctrine, and more widely accepted standards.

The Reformation restored understanding of justification by faith and direct access to God through Yeshua, without the need for other intermediaries. The superior and ultimate authority of Scripture was also foundational. The Reformation embraced the ideal found in this oft-used expression: "In essentials unity, in non-essentials liberty, and in all things charity."

Up to this point the basic thrust of the Reformation and its effects were still orientated against fragmentation. While Lutheran and Reformed churches did not embrace the apostolic succession doctrine of authority as did the Anglicans, they still embraced a form of government where leaders had to be ordained by other ordained leaders, so a succession and order of some significant type was maintained.

Post-Reformation Movements

Post-Reformation movements generally maintained a concern for the unity of the Church, not only as an invisible reality, but as something to be manifested in the unity of doctrine and the government of the churches. What prevented this unity were differences in deep convictions. Strongly held beliefs precluded association with others who did not hold exactly the same convictions. An exception was in the Congregationalists, who saw the churches as voluntary associations of individuals in a local setting or gathering. This form of understanding would influence a great number of Baptists.

Generally, those who sought new reforms sought to do so within existing church bodies. The movement of Pietism in the Lutheran Churches maintained unity with the Lutheran denomination. In addition, the Methodist movement under Wesley maintained unity with the Anglicans, though the Anglicans made it difficult. The great reforms of Wesley included public preaching and personal commitment to Messiah as central, and small group bands as centers for discipleship and the raising of leaders. This was the "method." The Anglicans could not allow for a parallel lay leadership structure that Wesley promoted. Hence, after Wesley died, Methodists were largely forced out.

The Methodists were correct in their controversy with the Anglicans, as shown by their extraordinary effect on world evangelism and missions. Their practical methods produced church planting at unprecedented levels. The Church today would benefit greatly from this kind of thinking. Unity is achieved much faster by the practical application of commitment to other believers than it is by argument and debate.

I want to especially note the orientation of the reform movements we have emphasized to this point. Most were committed, if possible, to stay within the bodies in which they were found. They wanted to practice truths and methods that they saw as a restoration or recovery of biblical truth. In conviction, they believed they had to practice the truth that was revealed to them. They believed themselves to be forced out by being denied these convictions. So the Lutherans were forced out, as were the Reformed and Methodist movements.

Some were troubled at the beginnings of fragmentation. The most noteworthy, Count Ludwig Von Zinzendorf, was one of the greatest leaders of Protestant Church history. In my view, Zinzendorf and his community were the foreshadowing figures of where the Church needs to go in our own day.

Zinzendorf was part of the Pietism movement in the German Lutheran Church. He formed a community for spiritual life, unity, prayer, and world missions. He is famous for launching a 24-hour prayer watch that lasted for 100 years, and is considered the father of Protestant world missions. Zinzendorf's commitment to unity established a key principle in his community called Hernhutt. Any truly committed Christian could be part of it—Lutheran, Reformed, or Catholic.

When the Moravians approached Zinzendorf to lead them, he sought God's guidance. The Moravians were a reformation movement in Bohemia, today the area of the Czech Republic and Slovakia. They were almost destroyed by the persecution of the Hapsburg-Catholic leadership. Zinzendorf accepted the Moravian invitation.

The Moravians believed in apostolic succession. Zinzendorf accepted this doctrine. Under his leadership, the Moravians became a world movement and were a key influence on the Methodists. Zinzendorf would only plant a Moravian church where the Moravian missionary could not bring unity to the other Protestants already planted in a particular town. He sought the unity of Lutherans, Reformed and Anglican. He could say to the Lutherans, "We believe in justification by faith," to the Reformed, "We believe in eldership government," and to the Anglicans, that he embraced apostolic succession so that the bishop would lead the elders.[3]

Zinzendorf also embraced the election of ethnic Israel. This was deep commitment and we now know that his disciples planted the first Messianic Jewish Congregation since early post biblical times in the 1740s in Amsterdam. Even rabbis were secretly a part of this underground Messianic Jewish community.[4]

Sadly, Zinzendorf's ideals were not embraced by most. As we move to the nineteenth century, Protestants who believed that they discovered restoration truths were very willing to simply form new associations. In some cases, they sought to bring truth into existing denominations and were rebuffed and forbidden to practice their convictions, but in too many situations they were not forced out. However, this does not mean that truth was not being restored. For example, the healing movements at the end of the nineteenth century and the holiness movements led to new denominations as the Christian Missionary Alliance and the Nazarenes.

These movements formed a background for the Pentecostal movements that embraced the experience of the initial filling of the Holy Spirit (baptism in the Spirit) and the importance of the supernatural gifts of the Spirit. The great Pentecostal denominations were thus formed. Many of them (not Pentecostal Holiness) embraced a more Baptist or Congregationalist ideal of independent churches. The Black Pentecostals and Pentecostal Holiness had room for the idea of overseers or bishops.

Paradoxically, we find that the denominational movements were bringing emphases that were missing in the bodies from which they separated. On the one hand, they were a legitimate challenge concerning truths that were lost or not given their due.

On the other hand, it is difficult to see how the fragmentation into hundreds of denominations and independent churches with no accountability beyond themselves was a good thing. Peter Hocken noted that much of this comes from arrogance where the splitting group despises the original group and thinks they have replaced them, and that they are no longer legitimate. Dr. Hocken traces this to the attitudes of the Gentiles in the first church split, where the Gentiles rejected the Jewish church and embraced replacement theology with regard to Israel or the Jewish people.

The Western Church Today

Today fragmentation continues, especially in the West, and movements for unity are short lived. Much that was lost over many centuries through fragmentation is being restored, but the ideal of the One New Man is still to be achieved universally. In the majority church world, great movements are taking place both within, but even more outside of, traditional denominations. Especially in nations where persecution is common, there is a quest for unity and even a recognition of elders tying many churches together as one.

The formation of denominations is a mixed blessing. As noted earlier, steps toward fragmentation were generally the result of a desire to maintain and protect something of value in Church life. For example, the previously mentioned Donatist movement was a reaction to perceived corruption in the Church. Augustine's opposition to it was prompted by a healthy desire to prevent schism and maintain unity.

Denominations bring with them both good and bad. They have provided several benefits, such as restoring lost truths; providing a variety of expressions of faith tailored to individual tastes; and fresh expression for creativity and growth. At the same time, denominationalism has led to an ungodly competitive spirit and a lack of essential accountability from both laymen and leaders. The resulting lack of unity exposes the Church to accusations by enemies of the Gospel that there are no clear theologies or practices in the Bible and the Church is hypocritical. Thus, much of the Church's outreach is rendered ineffective.

The degree to which denominationalism is judged good or bad depends on how well we eliminate competitiveness and embrace the prayer of Yeshua for unity. When He prayed that his disciples would be one, He did not have in mind that they should all become exactly the same. Each individual brought value to the whole.

As the Church spread into other parts of the world, the degree of diversity increased exponentially. But in that diversity of culture and ethnicity, there was always the potential for unity on the basis of the same principles that made the early Church a model of how the Body of Believers should function. Regardless of individual differences, Yeshua desired oneness in faith and oneness in love, with appropriate honor given to the heritage and the foundation on which the Church began, as well as a sense of accountability to properly appointed leadership.

Those who see denominationalism as nothing more than evil should note that each step toward the fractioning of the Church was taken with the intention of protecting the unity and the purity of the Church. The evils of separation did not arise from intention, but rather from losing sight of the real goal that Yeshua had in mind when he prayed for unity.

When we speak of the prayer of Yeshua that they may be one, our minds easily connect to another passage, that God has broken down the wall of partition between Jew and Gentile and made them into One New Man. Expressing the unity of Jew and Gentile is a key to the unity of the churches. Since the Church was birthed out from the Jewish people, the alignment of the Church with the Jewish people and the Messianic Jewish part of it is easily seen as a spiritual necessity of honoring where honor is due.

The unity of Jew and Gentile is shown in the New Testament to not be a unity of homogenization, but a unity that preserves the distinctive destiny and calling of each. Acts 15, 21. and First Corinthians 7 make this abundantly clear.

Too often those who have called for unity have called for conformity. The idea of unity in diversity is the key to preserve the values of the varieties of cultures among different peoples. Those cultural varieties must be purged, by discarding what is incompatible with the Scriptures. However, God wills variety. R. Kendall Soulen in his great book, *The God of Israel and Christian Theology*, makes a passionate and convincing case for this orientation.

The unity of the Church should also be a challenge to Messianic Jews to embrace all social forms that foster Jewish life in Yeshua, whether Messianic Jewish congregations or Jewish fellowships (*chavarot*) that are part of larger churches. Yes, the social reinforcement to live a Jewish life is crucial to attain it. It is important to realize that much of Jewish life and practice is a corporate matter and that individualism as a way of Jewish life alone will not do.

A key to unity is that the churches will embrace the truth that Jews who come to faith in Yeshua are called to live and identify as part of their people. Those who are Jewish and who claim that the Gentile church is not part of their heritage need to revisit and reevaluate those convictions.

At the same time, those Gentiles who are convinced that the Jewish roots of their Christian beliefs are not important must also think again. Yeshua was and is the Jewish Messiah. It is impossible to understand the scope of the Church's mission without understanding that foundation.

Endnotes

1. J.N.D. Kelly, *Early Christian Doctrines* (New York; Harper, 1978), pp. 3-28.

2. Oscar Skarsaune, *In the Shadow of the Temple* (Downers Grove: InterVarsity Press, 2002).

3. Weinlick, John R., and Fred Bees, *Count Zinzendorf* (Bethlehem, PA: Moravian Publications, 1956).

4. Pastor Bender and Archdeacon Johannes Fichetenbauer, Toward Jerusalem Council II Power Point, based on archival studies, Vienna, 2001.

CHAPTER 6

Celebrating Our Distinctives and Honoring the Body: Two Divine Keys to Spiritual Unity[1]

Dr. Michael L. Brown, ICN Ministries, Founder

The Lord saved me in an Italian Pentecostal church at the end of 1971. At that time I was a proud, rebellious, heroin-shooting, LSD-using, rock-drumming, 16-year-old Jew with no interest in God and no faith in Jesus, but through the medium of this small and unpretentious congregation, I was gloriously born anew. I am forever grateful to those devoted, faithful saints who put up with my foolishness and prayed me into the kingdom.

In those first years in the Lord, the divine fellowship I experienced on a regular basis was wonderfully sweet. I understood what Peter meant when he wrote about *"joy unspeakable and full of glory"* (1 Pet. 1:8 KJV). And passion for the Word, for spiritual service, for winning the lost, for prayer, was the norm, to the point that, by early 1972, I was spending at least six hours a day alone with God: at least three hours in prayer, at least two hours reading the Word, and one solid hour memorizing Scripture (committing 20 verses a day to memory without fail).

But my spirituality reflected both the strengths and weaknesses of the congregation, and to the extent that we were deeply devoted to the Lord, we were also extremely narrow. *We* had the pure doctrine; *we* had the right teaching; *we* were special—and this appealed to me. I loved being right!

One time I asked the pastor's wife (who was the daughter of the founding pastor), "How did we get such pure doctrine?" She explained to me that her husband, the pastor, got it from her father.

In hushed tones, I asked, "And where did *he* get such pure doctrine?" She replied, "He got it from the elders."

This led me to ask with reverential awe, "And where did the elders get such pure doctrine?"

"They got it straight from God!" she replied.

Extraordinary! I really *was* in the right place.

Not long after this, I became interested in Dispensationalism, which was taught strongly by our pastor. I was determined to master the ins and outs of the pre-trib rapture, a doctrine that, I had to admit, I had not learned while poring through the Scriptures on my own. So, I purchased some of the classic expositions of the subject, learned that the seventh (and last) trumpet in Revelation 11 was not the same as the last trumpet in First Corinthians 15, discovered how every detail of the end times was clearly spelled out in the Bible, and held to the doctrine with dogmatic tenacity.

How good it felt to be right, especially when I could back up my positions with a rapid-fire recitation of verses from all over the Bible, and how little tolerance I had for those who were unsure of what the Bible actually said about the end of the age.

One time, a woman in the Christian group at our college campus invited her pastor to talk with us about eschatology, and I remember being distinctly unimpressed with him. First, he didn't seem "anointed." (If I recall, he may have even been wearing a clerical collar!) Second, and more important, he presented various end-time views and cautioned against dogmatism. How dare he be so wishy-washy when the Bible was so clear!

As soon as the talk was over, I proceeded to confront him on his waffling position, explaining that the Bible was quite plain about the details of the return of Jesus, and that Dispensationalism was not one of several potential views. It was the only view. Needless to say, he was not particularly impressed with my narrow-minded, uncharitable approach.

Within three years, I had reversed my position, concluding that Dispensationalism was *not* biblical, recognizing that I had learned the system by reading dispensationalist books rather than by studying the Word. Of course, I now thought that I was right again (I'm sad to say that sometimes it takes me a while to "get it"), but with this shift in my position, some of the foundations of my dogmatism and narrow-mindedness were beginning to be undermined. Added to this was my increasing exposure to the larger Church world, which taught me that there were a lot more views to be considered than I had previously imagined—and these varied views were held by godly teachers of the Word. Perhaps I had wrongly judged them?

To be sure, there are spiritual and doctrinal hills on which I am prepared to die. I am absolutely committed to salvation in and through Jesus alone. In other words, the way to life *is* narrow (see Matt. 7:13-14; Luke 13:23-24) and Yeshua's name remains the one name through which we must be saved (see Acts 4:12). I am absolutely committed to the Great Commission (see Matt. 28:18-20; Luke 24:46-49; see also Mark 16:15-18), believing that our Savior shed His blood for the world and that it is our sacred duty to bring this good news to the ends of the earth.

I am absolutely committed to scriptural holiness, being convinced that Jesus died not only to save us from hell but to save us from sin (see Matt. 1:23), that holiness is our destiny (see Eph. 1:4) and our calling (see 1 Pet. 1:14-19; Heb. 12:14), and that His goal is to have for Himself a beautiful bride, *"without stain or wrinkle or any other blemish, but holy and blameless"* (Eph. 5:27 NIV).

And I am absolutely committed to Yeshua's high priestly prayer that all of His followers be one (see John 17:20-23), and that requires humility and honor, a recognition of our interdependence, and an understanding that not one of us has it all or knows it all. We become the One New Man through our identity in Yeshua and the life He imparts to us, not through the perfect accuracy of every *jot* and *tittle* of our teaching. That's why Proverbs 3:7-8 has become a "life verse" for me: *"Do not be wise in your own eyes; fear the LORD and shun evil. This will bring health to your body and nourishment to your bones."*

God has a great big family, and none of us have every detail of our beliefs or practices right. To think that we do is the height of spiritual arrogance. To think that we do is to demean our brothers and sisters. This is the principle of being a "Body":

The eye cannot say to the hand, "I don't need you!" And the head cannot say to the feet, "I don't need you!" On the contrary, those parts of the body that seem to be weaker are indispensable, and the parts that we think are less honorable we treat with special honor. And the parts that are unpresentable are treated with special modesty, while our presentable parts need no special treatment. But God has combined the members of the body and has given greater honor to the parts that lacked it, so that there should be no division in the body, but that its parts should have equal concern for each other. If one part suffers, every part suffers with it; if one part is honored, every part rejoices with it. Now you are the body of Christ, and each one of you is a part of it (1 Corinthians 12:21-27 NIV).

In 1988, after bringing a controversial keynote message at a historic, Messianic Jewish gathering in Jerusalem, the Lord taught me another valuable lesson. Over the years, I had learned not to esteem myself more highly than I should, recognizing my own weaknesses and understanding that there were no superstars in the Body. But there was something I was missing: Not only is it sinful to over-esteem oneself, but it is sinful to *under-esteem* others, and that's exactly what I had done. I had negatively judged my fellow-leaders since they did not carry the same burden I carried or minister the same way I did. Rather than exalting myself, I subtly degraded them—not as people, but in terms of the importance of their callings—and the Lord dealt with me very deeply about this. As Jesus famously said in Matthew 23:8, *"But you are not to be called 'Rabbi,' for you have only one Master and **you are all brothers"** (NIV).

Paul emphasized this truth in Romans 12:

Just as each of us has one body with many members, and these members do not all have the same function, so in Christ we who are many form one body, and each member belongs to all the others…. Live in harmony with one another. Do not be proud…. Do not be conceited" (Romans 12:4-5,16 NIV).

This is one of the glorious principles of the "one new man," the principle of unity in diversity, the principle of a tapestry deriving its wholeness and beauty from the many different threads and colors and stitches. I came to appreciate this richness through the tapestry of congregations and ministries in which I served during the past four decades.

From 1971 to 1977, I was part of the aforementioned Italian Pentecostal church, then from 1977 to 1983, I served in a non-charismatic (or, barely charismatic), Reformed, socially conscious church (which did, however, experience a powerful outpouring the last months I was there), after which I taught at a Long Island branch of Christ for the Nations Institute from 1983 to 1987 while also attending (at times, grudgingly) a Word of Faith church. Then, from 1987 to 1993 I served in a flagship Messianic Jewish congregation in Maryland, leading the theological institute there while also preaching frequently at Times Square Church in Manhattan from 1991 to 1995. After this, I was called to serve on the leadership team of the Brownsville Revival from 1996 to 2000, pioneering the Brownsville Revival School of Ministry, which then became FIRE School of Ministry in 2001. (As an interesting footnote, I should mention that Brownsville Assembly of God was thoroughly dispensational in its theology!)

From 1986 until now, I have also ministered overseas on more than 100 trips in a total of 25 countries, including 20 trips to Italy, 16 trips to India, 12 or so trips each to Germany, Korea, and England, and 8 trips to Israel. In other words, I have been confronted with cultural diversity along with theological diversity and diversity in praxis, and sometimes the differences were quite jarring. On my first trip to India in 1993, as we arrived at the meeting place after more than two days of travel, I was distressed to hear the use of "demonic" sounding worship songs. What else could you call songs that were sung to the same melodies that were chanted in Hindu temples? I quickly learned that the music was wonderfully anointed, the words were incredibly powerful, and the "demonic" sounds were simply Indian tunes. So much for my discernment!

Over the course of these decades, my own views shifted from believing in divine healing (primarily because it was taught in the church in which I was saved), to questioning it (based on observation and skepticism), to firmly embracing it (based on intensive study of the Word); from Arminianism (having been saved in that theological environment), to Calvinism (largely due to intellectual study), to a rejection of Calvinism (due to a fresh encounter with God in a time of personal revival)—not to mention my changing views on Messianic Judaism, congregational leadership, and a host of other issues.

But I am far from uncertain in terms of running the race the Lord has assigned me. I am focused, committed, and determined not to deviate one iota from the path that has been set before me, regardless of cost or consequences.

This, however, seems to present a contradiction. How can we be committed to our particular calling within the Body without denigrating others? Or, conversely, how can we rightly esteem others without diluting the specificity and certainty or our own calling? A simple analogy will prove helpful.

Let's say that you are a flutist playing in a famous orchestra, but you are convinced that flutes are the only legitimate instrument. After all, flutes are silver and shiny, played delicately with lips and fingers—not like those violins and cellos, which are played with bows and can make such unpleasant sounds. And certainly not like those booming timpani drums, which are struck with a mallet. Flutes are *the* real instrument.

Obviously, this would be foolish and immature thinking, not the kind of thinking that would be conducive to a successful orchestra. After all, who ever heard of an all-flute orchestra? And so, upon reflection, you go to the opposite extreme. "I must make my flute sound like a violin or cello! I will learn to play it with a bow. On occasion I will even strike it with a mallet!"

This way of thinking, although humble, is perhaps even more destructive to the good of the orchestra, since you are no longer able to contribute what you are called to contribute. The distinctive sound of the flute is now missing.

What then is the right approach? Simply this: Because you know that you are a vital part of the orchestra, you will become the best flute player you possibly can, sharpening your craft until your flute part absolutely shines, but all the while recognizing that you are only one part of the orchestra, that your role is no more important than anyone else's, that all the musicians must follow the directions of the conductor. Yet if your fail to perform to your very best, the whole orchestra will be hurt.

Spiritually speaking, this means that you must run your race with every bit of strength you have, refusing to compromise your sacred convictions and giving yourself without reservation to the specific calling of God. At the same time, however, you are rooting for everyone else to succeed in his or her calling, recognizing that only together can we see the Lord fully glorified in the earth. We are more dependent on each other than we realize (or care to realize), and we are each more limited in scope than we tend to understand.

This means that, when we do differ on nonessentials of the faith (meaning, those areas that fall within the pale of orthodoxy), we do so with respect, and we do our best not to make judgments on outward appearances but on truth (see John 7:24). And we strive to recognize the unique gifts and contributions of our brothers and sisters in other camps, even if we are unable to work closely with them because of the depths of differences that might exist between us.

As I have frequently told our ministry students, "There might be a church down the block that is cessationist, holds to replacement theology, is hierarchically structured in its leadership, and believes in once-saved, always-saved [none of which we hold to in our school], and yet if you serve there for a season, you will learn something of value for the Kingdom, and you'll find that they have unique strengths or insights that we are lacking." I honestly believe this to be true.

Recently, I was lecturing on Jeremiah at a local seminary, talking about the destructive effects of false prophets, when one of the students asked me, "What about false prophets today?"—and he proceeded to name some of these contemporary "false prophets," one of whom was a good friend of mine at whose Bible school I had also taught!

How then can I serve in both schools? The key is to recognize the genuine devotion to the Lord of each school's leadership, to embrace the distinct calling of each school, and to understand the nature of the contribution I can make to each of these schools. If I can do that without compromising my integrity or convictions, and if the leaders are willing to embrace me for who I am, then there is no conflict. In fact, there is freedom. Why? *It is because I am not there to change those schools into my image but rather to contribute into their unique image the specific things the Lord has given to me.*

Think of it like this. Let's say you are an expert cook with a strong marketing background as well, and you have a vision to bring together all the different ethnic foods in your city. Do you call in the finest Mexican and Italian and American and Chinese and French and Japanese chefs, ask them to prepare some of their best meals, and *then mix all the meals together*? Certainly not!

Rather, you devise a plan in which each chef prepares his or her very best ethnic menu, you work with them to produce the finest meals at the best prices, and then you open up a big food court featuring all the different restaurants. And there you have it: unity in diversity; everyone eating in the same place; everyone satisfying their own distinct tastes; some people trying new dishes—and all this without making Egg Foo Young Parmesan or Sushi Tamales. Let the flavors be distinct!

I once taught a class at FIRE School of Ministry on doctrinal differences, giving the students principles that would help them sort through issues that tend to polarize God's people. And when we reviewed the four major end-time views (dispensational premillennialism; historic premillennialism; postmillennialism; and amillennialism), we were able to glean important truths from each view (respectively, we must emphasize the return of Jesus; we must recognize that the promises to Israel will be literally fulfilled; we must believe that the Gospel will triumph in the earth; and we must understand that Jesus is currently reigning over His spiritual kingdom). The fact that I hold to historic premillennialism does not mean that I see all other views as theological and scripturally bankrupt. Perhaps my dissenting brother has something to teach me after all?

In keeping with this attitude, I labor day and night with the deep understanding that I do not have it all and I do not know it all. At the same time, I am profoundly aware that if I fail to do my part—if I fail to sound the alarm when danger is near, if I fail to stand boldly for truth when others are caving in, if I fail to equip and teach in the areas where I have been given expertise—then I am not only dishonoring the Lord but I am hurting the rest of the Body.

Let us honor one another in humility and respect, and let each of us do our part with passion and conviction. We really do need each other!

Without this understanding, we will not function effectively as "One New Man," nor will we impact the world as we are called to do.

But if each of us, Gentile and Jew together and in our distinctive callings, will recognize the handiwork of the Lord in mutual honor and particular obedience, then the world will have no name for us other than "those Jesus people," just as, at Antioch, the joint assembly of believing Jews and Gentiles were first called "Christians" (or, "Messianics"; see Acts 11:26). As Darrell Bock noted,

The name is significant because it shows that it was the identification with Jesus as the Christ, as the Messiah, that people noticed. It also suggests that a separate identity is emerging for this group which earlier was appealing to Jews only...[2]

Certainly this is included in Yeshua's prayer, *"May they be brought to complete unity to let the world know that You sent Me and have loved them even as You have loved Me"* (John 17:23). And certainly this expression of unity can only come through the respectful recognition of each part of the Body and the celebration of our unity in diversity:

> *For just as the body is one but has many parts; and all the parts of the body, though many, constitute one body; so it is with the Messiah* (1 Corinthians 12:12 JNT).

Endnotes

1. When I received the invitation to contribute a chapter to this volume, it was suggested that the chapter be based more on my life experiences than on a detailed exegesis of biblical texts, hence the highly personal nature of this contribution.

2. Darrell L. Bock, *Acts* (Grand Rapids, MI: Baker Exegetical Commentary, 2007), 416.

CHAPTER 7

Ruth and Naomi: A Model of Reconciliation and Redemption

Sandra Teplinsky, Light of Zion, Co-President

(Adapted from *Israel's Anointing*, by Sandra Teplinsky, published by Chosen Books, used by written permission of Baker Publishing Group.)

For he himself is our peace, who has made the two one and has destroyed the barrier, the dividing wall of hostility... His purpose was to create in himself one new man out of the two, thus making peace, and in this one body to reconcile both of them to God through the cross (Ephesians 2:14-16 NIV).

An unprecedented move of the Spirit, destined to increase in coming years, is the global rejoining of Gentile to Jewish believers in Messiah. In 1975, only a dozen or so established Messianic congregations were known to exist in the world. At this writing less than 40 years later, some estimate that up to half a million Jews follow Jesus.[1] Of these, most are in mainstream churches. Others affiliate either with Messianic congregations or house-type fellowships. Some undoubtedly keep their faith secret.[2]

Like estranged family members reunited after too many years apart, Gentile and Jewish believers are at long last becoming reacquainted—joyously, but not without occasional stretch or strain. Each is restoring to the other essential dimensions of the Kingdom of God and the knowledge of His ways. In the process, the whole Body is being given opportunity to mature in love.

The concept of Jews and Gentiles together, in Christ as "One New Man," is articulated in the book of Ephesians. In context, it flows from the broad description of God's redemptive plan from before creation. The One New Man is not an isolated phenomenon. We exist and function within a much larger Kingdom reality than simply Jews and Gentiles getting along well together—though that is an important start. God's stupendous plan is to bring *all things* in heaven and on earth together under Messiah's government of love, *"that in the coming ages, he might show the incomparable riches of his grace...in Christ Jesus"* (Eph. 2:7 NIV). Deity's dominion, which knows no end, showcases His unparalleled, rich grace forever, to His good pleasure. Within this larger Kingdom context, non-Jewish believers are *"no longer foreigners and aliens, but fellow citizens with God's people."* They are *"heirs together with Israel, members together of one body"* (Eph. 2:19; 3:6). Let's look at the blessing and glory that results.

One New Humanity in the Book of Ruth

Throughout the Bible, people from all nations are invited to worship Israel's God. We learn of Abraham's servant Eliezer; a "mixed multitude" leaving Egypt in the Hebrew exodus; Moses' Gentile wife Zipporah and father-in-law Jethro; Rahab of Jericho; and converts from King Xerxes' empire during Esther's day. In the New Covenant, God-fearing Gentiles worship in synagogues even before the Gospel is preached to them. Then, through Jesus, the door to the Kingdom opens even wider to whoever, wherever, believes in Him. The Scriptures refer to this transcendent phenomenon of Jew and Gentile as One New "Man." (Because the meaning is identical, I generally prefer the translation "humanity.")

The early Church, which was mostly Jewish, quickly discerned that nationality alone did not confer spiritual standing before God. There is neither Jew nor Greek, slave nor free, male nor female when it comes to partaking of the blessings of salvation (see Gal. 3:28). These distinctions, of course, still exist in the earth realm. They bear upon our daily lives and, to some extent, our redemptive destinies.[3] But they are not relevant to our sanctification or status in God's Kingdom.

To help flesh out reconciliation between Jews and Gentiles in Christ, two biblical heroines of the faith, our elder sisters Ruth and Naomi, serve as vivid prototypes. The unswerving devotion of the Gentile Ruth to the Jewish Naomi, together with Naomi's sacrificial deference to Ruth, offers us a revelatory glimpse into the matchless mystery of One New Humanity. The serendipitous tale demonstrates how Jew and Gentile together, serving one another in a relationship of mutual love, proved instrumental to Yeshua's first coming. Assuredly, it will again take Jew and Gentile together, each preferring the other in divine reciprocity, to bring about His Second Coming.

Interestingly, observant Jews read the entire book of Ruth every year during the Levitical feast of Shavuot. Shavuot celebrates the first fruits of Israel's agricultural harvest. It was on Shavuot that, over 2,000 years ago, the Holy Spirit rained down on dozens of followers of Yeshua. As a result, the New Covenant Church was born. This unparalleled event, ushering in the first fruits of Israel's spiritual harvest among the nations, came to be known as Pentecost. The mystery of One New Humanity—Jews and Gentiles in Messiah—began to unfold. Little wonder the

Jewish people, whether or not they fully understand why, honor noble Ruth on this day.

Israel's Desolation

The book of Ruth is primarily a Spirit-breathed, literal account of historical events.[4] But it also constitutes a typology or prophetic allegory befitting the twenty-first-century Church. The narrative takes place approximately 3,000 years ago. In the opening scene, an Israelite named Elimelech, his wife, Naomi, and their two sons leave home to escape a famine. As you may know, names in the Scriptures are significant, reflecting the characteristics and callings of persons and places. In Ruth, names bespeak much of the book's prophetically instructive message, and deserve some attention.

The name Elimelech means "My God is King," while Naomi translates into "Pleasant." The couple has two sons, Mahlon, meaning "Weak," "Sickly," or "Afflicted," and Kilion, meaning "Wasting Away." The family belongs to the clan of Ephrathites, which means "Fruitful Ones." They come from Bethlehem, or "House of Bread," which is located in Judah, meaning "Praise." So at the outset, we know we have met a fruitful family called to nourish others. But there is a famine in the land, and so their offspring are weak, sickly, afflicted, and wasting away.

Famine in the Scriptures represents a form of judgment. We need not delve too deeply to know that the story transpired during a time of rebellion against God. The first sentence in Ruth tells us the events took place "in the days when the judges ruled." The book of Judges, which immediately precedes Ruth, concludes with this sorry remark: *"In those days Israel had no king; everyone did as he saw fit"* (Judg. 21:25 NIV). The famine was deserved, and it was devastating.

Times being so trying, Elimelech and his family seek refuge in the land of Moab—Israel's longstanding enemy. Moab, meaning "From Father," was the son resulting from an incestuous union between Lot and one of his daughters (see Gen. 19:33-37). Despite their dubious ancestry, Moab's descendants grew into a prosperous nation. But they were cruel to Israel, and consequently, God cursed them:

> No…Moabite or any of his descendants may enter the assembly of the LORD, even down to the tenth generation. For they did not come to meet you [Israel] with bread and water on your way when you came out of Egypt, and they hired Balaam…to pronounce a curse on you" (Deuteronomy 23:3-4 NIV).

Moab was not the sort of sanctuary you would think a starving Jewish family from the Province of Praise would pick. It seemed the Moabites had forgotten that their very existence as a people, as well as their land, was due to the generosity of the progenitor of the Jews, namely Abraham. Recall that it was Abraham who ceded the most lush land in Canaan to Lot. Years later, it was Abraham's relationship with him that resulted in Lot and his family's deliverance from the brimstone annihilation of Sodom and Gomorrah. But as the years passed, so did any sense of kinship on the part of Moab's descendants with Abraham's covenant children. Could the same be said, perhaps, of some in the Church—in relation to Israel?

Nonetheless, Moab finds itself hosting a displaced Jewish family of destiny. There the head of the household, Elimelech ("My God is King"), dies. It is as if the kingship of God is no more for this family. Sons Mahlon and Kilion marry Moabite women, but, being the weak, sickly, afflicted and wasting away souls that they are, these two young men also die, and without children. The family's attempt to escape judgment has failed, and as a result,

Naomi is "Pleasant" no longer. Soon she will change her name to Mara, meaning "Bitter."

Meanwhile, news arrives that Israel's famine has come to an end. The season of judgment is over; Naomi decides to go home. She bids her two daughters-in-law a difficult farewell. Blessing them both, she urges them to stay in Moab, make new lives, find new husbands, and start new families. At this, the young women are genuinely distressed. They weep together in protest and grief. But then Orpah, whose name means "Back of the Neck," says goodbye and departs. Turning the back of her neck to her mother-in-law, she goes *"back to her people and her gods"* (Ruth 1:15).

Crossroads for the Church

In contrast, Ruth, whose name means "Friend" or "Clinging One," will not be dissuaded. Instead she clings all the more tenaciously to Naomi. Ruth utters words that have come to represent a commitment so supreme as to find place in many marriage vows today:

> *Where you go I will go, and where you stay I will stay. Your people will be my people and your God my God. Where you die I will die, and there I will be buried. May the LORD deal with me, be it ever so severely, if anything but death separates you and me* (Ruth 1:16-17 NIV).

At this juncture, the book's allegorical symbolism sharpens into focus. We see that Naomi personifies Israel as a whole, God's "pleasant" people. But just as Naomi becomes Mara when the living presence of God as King is removed from her, so does Israel's pleasantness turn bitter without Him.

Israel today, like other nations, has not collectively surrendered to God. As in the book of Judges and time of Ruth, the twenty-first-century Jewish state has no king, and in a sense, everyone does as he sees fit. Millennia of murderous persecutions, a century of terror, and ceaseless threats of annihilation have also taken their toll. For these and other reasons, Israel again endures a type of pervasive spiritual famine. But the story is not over. The suffering of the Jewish nation will be used by Yahweh for something ultimately far grander than she, like Naomi, could imagine.

Ruth, meanwhile, portrays Gentile Christians from the nations who have so joined themselves to Israel and her God that they cannot, under any circumstance, return to Moab or their Moabite gods. Ruth's choice to stick with embittered Naomi, come what may, turns on two firmly resolved matters. First, she is thoroughly devoted to Yahweh. Second, because of her faithfulness to Him, she sincerely and unconditionally loves her mother-in-law. In other words, she identifies fully with the family into which she has married. In so doing, Ruth depicts Christians who fully identify with the family of their Jewish Bridegroom-King.

Orpah, on the other hand, decides differently. At first, hers seems the more sensible choice. But Orpah depicts Christians who, in crisis, revert to the security and society of the world. She can be seen as representing those who fall from faith in times of shaking, trial, and tribulation.

The opposite choices made by the two daughters-in-law portentously parallel those we will make as believers today. As with Orpah and Ruth, our decisions will affect our destinies. Like them, Gentile believers have joined themselves by faith to the God of Israel. They have reaped blessing through the Jewish Scriptures, as well as through the Jewish patriarchs, prophets, apostles, and Messiah—through whom they have married, so to speak, into a Jewish family.

The two Moabite women come to a crossroads. To continue on with God in the totality of what He has for them, they must cling to Naomi. The alternative is not to go forward in Him at all, but back to familiar gods of the world. Similarly, in these last days, the true Body of Christ will cling tenaciously to Israel. To go forward in God in the years ahead, we must, like Ruth, go forward with Israel—or we shall not genuinely go forward at all. Such is the calling of the last days' Bride for which Messiah is coming (see Rev. 19:7).

Those radically in love with their Bridegroom-King will love His Jewish people. Having touched the inner chambers of God's heart, their own hearts will resonate to His yearning for His ancient ones. Most wholly in love with the Most Holy, the Bride will prove so resolute in courage as to advance headlong, like Ruth, into a future fraught with uncertainty. Dependent entirely on God, she'll willingly be escorted by a covenant counterpart who, like Naomi, will seem at times a bit more bitter than pleasant.

Catch the full extent of young Ruth's valiant humility. From a rather sordid background and cursed family lineage, she refuses to let her past impede her future. Ruth may or may not know that God's curse on Moab—lasting ten generations—is likely just now ending. What she does know is that God is worth everything. Those of us with personal or family histories of dysfunction can take heart. The past prevails no more when He is our Chief Goal.

Here I would like to share a side note with fellow Jewish believers in Yeshua. Years ago, I realized I did not fit neatly into any category represented by the cast of characters portrayed in Ruth. So I asked the Lord, "Are Messianic Jews Ruth, or are we Naomi?" The answer came clearly: "Yes... You are Rumi." The Spirit was saying we're to make room to humbly embrace and embody the exemplary characteristics of both Ruth and Naomi. He wants us joyfully appropriating and lovingly modeling His grace for roomy hearts and lives toward both covenant peoples.

Gleaning Blessings

Resuming the biblical tale, Ruth and Naomi set out for Beth-lehem, where their arrival generates a veritable stir. Elimelech's widow has changed so much that she is barely recognizable to her countrymen. Plus, she has brought with her an unenviable Moabi-tess. Naomi bemoans, *"The LORD has afflicted me; the Almighty has brought misfortune upon me"* (Ruth 1:21 NIV).

In recent years, Naomi's groan has been shared by many in Israel. It echoes each time another Jewish life is ravaged by yet another terror attack, or unjust international condemnation is issued, or genocidal threat hurled at the beleaguered sliver of a state. Yet this groaning of the country's corporate soul, like Naomi's, reflects an abiding—albeit perplexed—awareness that somehow God is still involved. Israel's groan will not dissuade Christians who, in the spirit of Ruth, refuse to let go of the Jewish people because they know it's alongside them that God's richest blessings will be found. The closer we come to Messiah's return, the greater the convergence of His two covenant peoples. In the process, unredeemed Israel will increasingly discover that her salvation and her Savior manifest through His saintly ones.

The last days Bride will be a radical firebrand provoking Israel to envy for her Messiah. According to Romans 11:11, *"Salvation has come to the Gentiles to make Israel envious."* For almost 2,000 years, this mandate has gone largely unfulfilled. But when the Jewish people encounter a company of militant lov-ers in whose midst Yeshua dramatically dwells, many of them will see Him at last—and they will reclaim their Desired of all Nations (see Hag. 2:7).

That is not all. The revelation of One New Humanity in the book of Ruth subtly suggests more. Though time and space permit only the briefest mention of the matter, it is no coincidence that the book's key characters are female. A glorious last days' gender reconciliation will take place in Messiah's corporate Bride. This restoration of humankind's very first divide is requisite to Jews and Gentiles attaining to full maturity as one in Christ.[5]

Meanwhile, returning to Ruth, we find the timing of Naomi's homecoming proves providential. It happens to be harvest season—and what better place to find food than in the House of Bread (Bethlehem)? Prophetically, Ruth's emergence in Israel at harvest season corresponds to the Church's embrace of the Jewish nation as part of the end times' spiritual harvest. Now, in Ruth's day, even the most needy could find food during a harvest, for with the season came the opportunity to glean. Gleaning was God's merciful form of social welfare whereby designated portions of crops were left for the poor to gather freely (see Lev. 23:22).

So back in Bethlehem, Ruth goes gleaning. The younger and presumably physically sturdier of the two, she undertakes the taxing job to nourish and sustain both Naomi and herself. Remarkably, from this point on Naomi never again refers to her as a daughter-in-law, but as "my daughter." Ruth is blessing Naomi as typically only a daughter (or son) would bless a mother, in covenant love and faithfulness. The profound significance of Ruth's sacrifice is more fully grasped when we consider that the Hebrew root-based definition of the word *bless* means to "kneel to enrich."[6] Ruth's kneeling in the sweltering, sun-baked fields of the Middle East to enrich Naomi offers a poignant picture of blessing.

God promises to bless those who bless Israel. Ruth, therefore, is about to glean a great deal more than grain. She quickly catches the eye of a chivalrous chap named Boaz, owner of the field in which she is studiously looking for leftovers. Tenderly he tells her,

> *My daughter, listen to me. Don't go and glean in another field and don't go away from here…. I have told the men not to touch you. And whenever you are thirsty, go and get a drink from the water jars the men have filled* (Ruth 2:8-9).

Ruth is honored, but baffled. We can imagine her mopping a sweaty brow, fingering sticky strands of hair from her face. *"Why have I found such favor in your eyes that you notice me—a foreigner?"* she asks (verse 10).

Boaz's reply reflects his own magnanimity of spirit:

I've been told all about what you have done for your mother-in-law since the death of your husband—how you left your father and mother and your homeland and came to live with a people you did not know before. May the LORD repay you for what you have done. May you be richly rewarded by the LORD, the God of Israel, under whose wings you have come to take refuge (Ruth 2:11-12).

Kinsman-Redeemer Comes in Strength

The Hebrew name Boaz means "In Him is Strength" or "Come (Now) in Strength." As it happens, Boaz is one of Naomi's relatives from Elimelech's side of the family. So when Ruth comes home and reports the day's good turn of events, Naomi is elated. She exclaims, *"That man is our close relative; he is one of our kinsman-redeemers"* (Ruth 2:20 NIV).

The role of kinsman-redeemer was prescribed in the Old Covenant Law (see Deut. 25:5-10). Certain relatives of a deceased Israelite were designated to protect the interests and inheritance of the surviving family. The kinsman-redeemer served, among other things, to father an heir for a brother who had died, thereby securing family property that would otherwise be lost due to death. But redemption by a kinsman—or his refusal to do so and his relegation of those duties to another—could only occur pursuant to specified procedures.

Naomi knows the rules. Learning of Boaz's benevolence toward Ruth, she dares to dream again. Suddenly we hear the pleasant/bitter one praising the Lord. "Could this Man be the hope of our redemption?" she perhaps thinks aloud. A strange flicker of faith—ignited by her Gentile daughter—sparks her soul. That flicker is about to explode into the surprise of a lifetime for Ruth, shaping history. Similarly, as Christians today bless Israel, the question will arise in Jewish hearts, *Could this Man—coming in strength—be the hope of our redemption?*[7]

Like Boaz of Bethlehem, Yeshua redeems all that was lost due to sin and death. And like Boaz, Yeshua is captivated by our clinging friendship to His Old Covenant people. His heart is won by believers from the nations demonstrating loving faithfulness to Israel. To all who trust in Him for salvation, He is revealed as Redeemer. But to those aligned with His kinfolk—His Jewish brethren according to the flesh—He reveals Himself as Kinsman, or Bridegroom. Indeed, the Bride's unconditional love for the Jewish nation helps make her ready for the soon coming King (see Matt. 25:40; Rom. 11:20b-21; Joel 3:1-2; Gen.12:3; Isa. 40:1-2; Rev. 19:7).

The Church's relationship with Israel, paralleling Ruth's relationship with Naomi, is ultimately about Messiah and following Him intimately. *"May you be richly rewarded by the LORD, the God of Israel, under whose wings you have come to take refuge,"* Boaz says in blessing the Moabitess (Ruth 2:12). Ruth has sought refuge not so much with Naomi as with Naomi's God. Now, the Hebrew word translated "wings" in this tender transaction can also refer to the corner of a garment or *tallit* (prayer shawl). Unconditional love for the Jewish nation is associated with coming under the Kinsman-Redeemer's *tallit*-like cover (see Ruth 3:9).

Divine Reciprocity

Up until now in the drama, Ruth has been the one kneeling to enrich Naomi. As a result, she has curried unexpected favor from a man possessing the potential to alter the course of her life. This, in turn, quickens Naomi's soul to the present reality of God in *her* life. Now it is Naomi who kneels to enrich Ruth—and beyond imagination.

According to the Law, Naomi herself, as surviving spouse of the deceased—not Ruth—inherits the right of kinsman-redemption (see Deut. 25:5; Ruth 4:5,9). Not only does Naomi have the legal right to Boaz, but he is much closer in age to her than to Ruth (see Ruth 3:10; 2:8). Surely he would make a terrific husband for the older, impecunious widow. Naomi has every common-sense reason to present herself to Boaz for marriage. Should he accept, her future would at last be secure. Even Ruth, it would seem, could stand to benefit. But this is not what Naomi chooses to do. Instead, she lays down her life for her friend.

Ruth can be redeemed only if Naomi voluntarily sacrifices her rights, and all the restorative blessings associated with them. Amazingly and without hesitation, this is precisely what she sets out to do. The matter is quickly resolved as far as Naomi is concerned. She approaches Ruth and says, *"My daughter, should I not try to find a home for you, where you will be well provided for?"* (Ruth 3:1).

Though embittered by life's hard blows, and perhaps all the more because of them, Naomi is extravagantly grateful for Ruth's loyalty and love. The young woman's steadfast devotion has transformed her, and she is able to reciprocate when the right time comes. With Ruth's best interest at heart, this consummate Jewish mother risks losing whatever she could possibly gain for her daughter's sake. For if Boaz redeems and marries Ruth, under normal circumstances Naomi is likely to fade from the scene. How probable is it a new bride will cling to a distressed, former mother-in-law once she has remarried into a prominent, upscale family?[8] Won't a new husband and future children eventually crowd her out? Naomi takes the chance.

In a certain sense, Israel has done for the Church what Naomi does here for Ruth. On a national level, Israel has deliberately—if unknowingly—forgone (temporarily) the blessings of redemption. As a result, salvation has come to the Gentiles. The Jewish people's corporate rejection of Kinsman-Redeemer Yeshua has meant the reconciliation of the world through Him (see Rom. 11:11,15). To the extent the Church benefits from unsaved Israel's national spurning of salvation in Messiah, the two covenant peoples of God resemble Ruth and Naomi at the deepest level of sacrifice at this juncture in the book.

Bear in mind that if Israel's recalcitrance has benefited the nations, her repentance will propel the world toward climactic blessing:

> *Moreover, if their stumbling is bringing riches to the world—*
> *that is, if Israel's being placed temporarily in a condition*
> *less favored than that of the Gentiles is bringing riches to*
> *the latter—how much greater riches will Israel in its full-*
> *ness bring them!.... For if their casting Yeshua aside means*
> *reconciliation for the world, what will their accepting Him*
> *mean? It will be life from the dead!* (Romans 11:12, 15 CJB[9])

Israel's redemption will mean nothing less than life from the dead. At its apex, Messiah will literally come to redeem and rule the earth. Recall that Yeshua conditioned His return on the Jews' repentant embrace of Him (see Matt. 23:39). As today's Ruth blesses today's Naomi, Naomi will bless Ruth in return. This back-and-forth synergy of relationship will escalate until blessing crescendos in the Person of the Kinsman-Redeemer who, like Boaz, comes in strength. For this divine, mutual reciprocity between Jew and Gentile, this exquisite interdependence and fruit thereof, the Bride will live and love and never give up. In so doing she prepares herself for the King.

Threshing Floor Test

Back in the Book of Ruth, matters are still at stake. If the Moabitess is to be redeemed, Naomi must carefully prepare her according to set ways and means. She therefore instructs Ruth scrupulously according to protocol. Her advice is not just kindly and motherly; any deviation from God's Word could backfire, dashing all their hopes to bits.

At first, Naomi's advice sounds reasonable: *"Wash and perfume yourself, and put on your best clothes"* (Ruth 3:3). But next it gets a little quirky and even kinky: *"Then go down to the threshing floor, but don't let him know you are there until he has finished eating and drinking. When he lies down…go and uncover his feet and lie down. He will tell you what to do"* (verses 3-4). That could sound, I daresay, downright scandalous.

We can assume that Ruth, who has demonstrated nothing less than stellar character, is a chaste woman of moral purity. Could she not have balked at Naomi's "teaching?" Might she have been tempted to conclude that these Jewish ways were getting a bit too bizarre for her? ("I've gone along with this 'Israel thing' up till now, but that's just not how we Gentiles do it…") But no—not missing a beat, she replies, *"I will do whatever you say"* (verse 5).

Naomi has surrendered her rights to Ruth; Ruth surrenders hers to Naomi. Divine reciprocity between Jew and Gentile is about mutual submission and humble service. There can be no arrogance or conceit on the part of Christians toward Israel (see Rom. 11:20-21,25). Just as certain, there is no place for Jewish pride toward Gentile believers. Any sense of self-importance will find itself exposed on a modern-day, metaphorical threshing floor. Recall that in ancient times, a threshing floor was the place where wheat was separated from chaff. Just as Ruth's embrace of her Jewish mother was tested on a threshing floor, there the Church's embrace of Israel will be tested, refined, and generously rewarded (see Matt. 3:12).

On that threshing floor, Ruth follows through on all she was told to do. We are allowed to eavesdrop on her encounter with Boaz—one that commences almost comically. According to the narrative,

> *In the middle of the night something startled the man, and he turned and discovered a woman lying at his feet. "Who are you?" he asked.*
>
> *"I am your servant Ruth," she said. "Spread the corner of your garment over me, since you are a kinsman-redeemer."*
>
> *"The LORD bless you, my daughter," he replied…. "I will do for you all you ask"* (Ruth 3:8-11).

Like Ruth, Gentile believers will emerge from their threshing floor test lavished with favor. It is there the Kinsman-Redeemer will spread over them the corner of His garment, His *tallit*. Their relationship with Him will be taken to new levels befitting His Bride.

Jew and Gentile Together Bring Redemption

Boaz readily fulfills all the requirements of the Law to complete Ruth's redemption, just as Jesus fulfilled all the requirements of the Law to redeem you and me. Then Boaz announces confidently to the community of Israel, *"I have bought…all the property of Elimelech, Kilion and Mahlon. I have also acquired Ruth the Moabitess, Mahlon's widow, as my wife"* (Ruth 4:9-10).

Boaz has rightfully been given all that belonged to Elimelech ("My God is King"), even as Yeshua has been given all things by our God who is King (see Eph. 1:22). Like Yeshua, Boaz has also rightfully taken all that belonged to "Weakness, Sickliness,

Affliction" (Mahlon), and "Wasting Away" (Kilion). As Israel and the Church join together in the spirit of Ruth and Naomi, they will be catapulted as One New Humanity into new dimensions of life, freed from the weakness, sickliness, affliction, and wasting away that have beset them both.

When Boaz claims Ruth as his, the whole community joyfully welcomes her in. No longer is Ruth a lowly foreigner. She is a full member of the household of Israel, the recipient of eternal esteem:

> *May the LORD make the woman who is coming into your home like Rachel and Leah, who together built up the house of Israel. May you have standing in Ephrathah and be famous in Bethlehem* (Ruth 4:11).

Like our forebears, we Messianic Jews must rejoice over, fully welcome, honor, and bless our redeemed brothers and sisters in Yeshua from the nations.

Blessings spoken over Ruth come to pass. In the closing scene of the book, she gives birth to a son named Obed ("Servant"). Obed becomes the grandfather of King David and a direct ancestor of Jesus the Messiah. Therefore, Obed's honored mother finds herself in the lineage of the Savior of humanity, her story preserved forever. She shines into infinity as the prototypical Gentile believer who partakes of all God's blessings of redemption because of her alignment with His Jewish people. She especially foreshadows the redeemed Arabic peoples destined to uniquely receive and mediate blessings to Israel and the nations.

Baby Obed, meanwhile, is nurtured by Naomi as if he were her own son. Obed ("Servant") serves to revive her to the extent she is pleasant again, shedding her name and identity as Mara or "Bitter" (see Ruth 4:16-17). By the fruit of Ruth's redemption, Naomi is in a sense brought back to life from the dead. According to the Hebrew text, she apparently nurses the babe at her own breast—a rare but verifiable phenomenon. She prophetically depicts Israel's response to Christian love. The Bride's relationship with the Incarnate Kinsman-Redeemer bears fruit that serves to revive Israel. Israel's revival in turn releases blessing that nurtures the nations.

One New Man Is a Bride

God used Jew and Gentile together to bring about Messiah's first coming. *So, too, it will take Jew and Gentile together, in the spirit of Ruth and Naomi, to bring about His Second Coming.* Israel will not turn to Yeshua and be saved without the love, intercession, and support of the international Church. This exquisite interdependence plays out in the mystery of One New Humanity—a mystery the Master is unraveling in our day.

The manifest reality of One New Humanity is destined to converge heaven with earth. But it will not go unopposed. As end times' birth pains intensify, opposition against Israel and the Jewish people will escalate exponentially, even among Christians. Only supernatural love will keep Jewish and Gentile believers united as one. Such love has but one Source: intimate communion with Yeshua the King. And such communion with Him is best described in a single word as bridal. When all is said and done, by glorious design, the One New Man is—a Bride.

Endnotes

1. Operation World, http://www.gmi.org/ow/country/isr/owtext.html. Other estimates are much lower; precise counts are impossible.

2. *Ibid.*

3. Israel's redemptive destiny means, for example, that she still retains the land covenant promised to Abraham, Isaac, and Jacob.

4. The Scriptures are to be interpreted first and foremost in a straightforward manner, based on the plain meaning of the biblical text in its grammatical-historical context, wherever it is reasonable to do so.

5. When God created man and woman, according to the Hebrew account, both were co-equally—as one—delegated dominion over the earth (see Gen. 1:26-28). Since the curse of the Fall, however, a peculiar war has raged between the devil and the daughters of Eve, inspired by Deity: *"I will put enmity between you [the serpent] and the woman, and between your offspring and hers; he will crush your head, and you will strike his heel"* (Gen. 3:15).

   "Woman" is fundamentally interpreted in a straightforward manner to mean literally, "woman." By the flesh and blood line of woman—not man—humanity would be redeemed. Accordingly, the devil has issues with women that he does not quite have with men. ("Woman" also prophetically refers to Israel, Miriam the mother of Yeshua, and the Church—but that is another, albeit intriguing, issue.)

   Is it possible that an unconscious enmity, echoing woman's prophetic mandate and redemptive role, resides in the collective human unconscious? If so, a certain parallel would exist between anti-Semitism and misogyny (hatred of women).

   The One New Man will in the last days restore and reconcile male and female, as well as Jew and Gentile, in Messiah. Humankind's original breach of divine covenant relationship—between man and woman—will be gloriously repaired through reciprocal, preferential love in grace. Ruth and Naomi give us a hint as to how.

6. James Strong, *The Exhaustive Concordance of the Bible, Main Concordance* (Nashville: Abingdon, 1977), see *bless* in Main Concordance and *barakh* in Hebrew and Chaldee Dictionary; Francis Brown, S.R. Driver and Charles A. Briggs, *A Hebrew and English Lexicon of the Old Testament* (Oxford: Clarendon Press, 1980), see *barakh*.

7. See Romans 11:26b, citing Isaiah 59:20 and 60:16; Matthew Henry, *Commentary on the Whole Bible*, http://www.ccel.org/h/henry/mhc2/Ru.ii.html.

8. Ruth's new mother-in-law could possibly have been Rahab, the harlot-turned-heroine of faith (see Matt. 1:5).

9. David H. Stern, *Complete Jewish Bible: An English Version of the Tanakh (Old Testament) and B'rit Hadashah (New Testament)* (Clarksville, Md.: Jewish New Testament Publications, 1998).

CHAPTER 8

The Master Plan for the One New Man

Jane Hansen Hoyt, Aglow International, President/CEO

**(excerpted and adapted from the book, *Master Plan*,
by Jane Hansen Hoyt)**

For He Himself is our peace, who has made the two one and has destroyed the barrier, the dividing wall of hostility, by abolishing in His flesh the law with its commandments and regulations. His purpose was to create in Himself one new man out of the two, thus making peace, and in this one body to reconcile both of them to God through the cross, by which He put to death their hostility. He came and preached peace to you who were far away and peace to those who were near. For through Him we both have access to the Father by one Spirit (Ephesians 2:14-18 NIV).

A God of Purpose

Before God said, *"Let there be light;"* before He said, *"Let there be a firmament;"* before God spoke the world into being, He had a plan. Just one plan—Plan A. No Plan B. No contingency in case things went wrong. No back-up. Just one plan that He would ensure would come to pass.

From Genesis to Revelation, it is clear that God is a God of eternal purpose. Job stated: *"I know that You can do everything, and that **no purpose of Yours** can be withheld from You"* (Job 42:2, emphasis mine).

In Isaiah 46:9-10, God says:

Remember the former things of old, for I am God, and there is no other; I am God, and there is none like Me, declaring the end from the beginning, and from ancient times things that are not yet done, saying, "My counsel shall stand, and I will do all My pleasure."

These words indicate to us that we can expect every prophetic purpose God has spoken since the beginning of time to be restored and fulfilled.

One of those prophetic purposes is stated in Ephesians 2:15 to create *"One New Man"*—Jew and Gentile—reconciled to each other and reconciled to God through the cross of Yeshua Messiah.

Four Key Words

There are key words for us in this passage. One is the word *peace*: Yeshua Himself is our peace and has broken down the wall of hostility, or the *"middle wall of separation"* (NKJV), between Jew and Gentile. That which separated, the Law and its commandment, was abolished "in his flesh."

The separation in the natural realm between Jew and Gentile, and in the spiritual realm, between men and God, was typified by the wall in the Temple dividing the court of the Gentiles from that of the Jews, and the veil in the Temple which separated all but the High Priest from the Holy of Holies. Yeshua, in his flesh, broke down that wall by fulfilling the Law and its requirements for peace with God and with each other.

One New Man is another key for us in this passage. When Yeshua died on the cross and rose again, He made the way for all the contention between Jew and Gentile to be removed so that a new spiritual body made up of both could be established—One New Man. He not only reconciles the two to each other, but actually incorporates both into one new body of believers. Faith in Yeshua and His completed work on the cross unites us and gives us a joined identity as the body of Messiah.

The third is *access.* Those who were "afar off," whether Jew or Gentile, have been *"brought near by the blood of Messiah"* (Eph. 2:13). The tearing of the veil in the Temple at Yeshua's death was a physical picture of the "access" to the Father that was made possible through His redemptive sacrifice. Under the Jewish law, only the high priest was allowed into the presence of God, and that only once a year when the proper sacrifice was offered. But under the "one new man" economy, every believer has the privilege of coming into the Holy of Holies (see Heb. 10:19-25). Jews and Gentiles now belong to the household of God and have access to the Father through the same spirit.

Reconcile is the fourth key word in this passage. Reconciliation sets God's people apart in a way that nothing else can.

One sign and wonder . . . that alone can prove the power of the Gospel is that of reconciliation... Hindus can produce as many miracles as any Christian miracle worker. Islamic saints in India can produce and duplicate every miracle that has been produced by Christians. But they cannot duplicate the miracle of black and white together, of racial injustice being swept away by the power of the Gospel... (Vinay Samuel).[1]

Reconciliation is a foundational doctrine of the Gospel. In the New Testament, the concept of reconciliation contains the idea "to change thoroughly" (Greek *katallasso*), "to change thoroughly from one position to another" (*apokatallatto*). Reconciliation, therefore, means that someone or something is completely altered and adjusted to a specific standard.[2] By the death of Messiah, the world is changed in its relationship to God. By the death of Messiah, Jew and Gentile are changed in their relationship to each other.

God's prophetic purpose revolves around unity. The goal of Plan A is bringing together, *"until we all reach unity in the faith and in the knowledge of the Son of God and become mature, attaining to the whole measure of the fullness of Messiah"* (Eph. 4:13 NIV). In His prayer for His disciples, Yeshua revealed the reason unity is so important: *"May they be brought to complete unity to let the world know that You sent Me and have loved them even as You have loved Me"* (John 17:23 NIV).

In Yeshua, we have peace instead of hostility, unity instead of separation, access to the Father and reconciliation with God and other people. In that reconciliation, *we know that we are loved by God.* The world, witnessing that love, has the opportunity to see the loving hand of God extended to them.

"It Is Not Good..."

The obvious challenge to unity is separation. Paul spoke in Ephesians 2 specifically about separation between Jew and Gentile, but in Galatians, he added to the list:

For you are all sons of God through faith in Messiah Yeshua.
For as many of you as were baptized into Messiah have put
on Messiah. There is neither Jew nor Greek, there is neither
slave nor free, there is neither male nor female; for you are
all one in Messiah Yeshua. And if you are Messiah's, then
you are Abraham's seed, and heirs according to the promise
(Galatians 3:26-29).

Reconciliation involves virtually every relationship known to human beings. As the "One New Man"—the body of Messiah—there will be no separation between Jew and Gentile, slave or free, male or female. We could add to that list any number of divided groups. In Messiah there is neither young nor old, rich nor poor, tall nor short.

This does not mean that faith in Messiah makes everyone the same. Jews do not stop being Jews when they become followers of Messiah. Gentiles do not stop being Gentiles. Faith in Messiah, however, eliminates the separateness. Jew and Gentile stand together in Messiah as equals joined by a common purpose and a common source of life.

Galatians tells us that the idea of unity, of breaking down the wall of separation, is not exclusively a matter of bringing together Jew and Gentile. That reconciliation is extremely important, as Scripture makes clear, but the problem of separation existed long before there was a distinction between Jew and Gentile. God identified separation as "not good" even before sin entered the world.

Genesis 1:31 tells us that when God finished the work of creation, He "saw everything that He had made, and *indeed it was very good*" (emphasis mine). He then created Adam (see Gen. 2:7) and gave him this instruction: *"Of every tree of the garden you may freely eat; but of the tree of the knowledge of good and evil you shall not eat, for in the day that you eat of it, you shall surely die"* (Gen. 2:16-17). In the next verse, God said, *"It is not good that the man should be alone; I will make him an help meet* **suitable** *for him"* (Gen. 2:18, KJV). Everything up to this point was "very good." But now, something was "not good."

What exactly was not good and why? Adam being *alone* seems to be the key thought in what God expresses here as "not good." The Hebrew word translated *alone* literally means "separation." Man was not merely lonely; his "separation" was of a spiritual nature. To me, it speaks of an inner aloneness. George Berry's *The Interlinear Literal Translation of the Hebrew Old Testament* translates Genesis 2:18 this way: "Not good is being the man to his separation."[3]

Even before the fall, separation was identified as a hindrance to man's purpose and God's plan. Adam had not yet been joined to God in His "divine life." For Adam to fulfill the purpose of God, he had to become a partaker of divine life. Adam would have to choose to receive divine life. Watchman Nee states in his book, *Messenger of the Cross*:

> Of all the edible trees, this one (the tree of life) is the most important. This is what Adam should have eaten first. Why is this so? The tree of life signifies the life of God, the uncreated life. Though at this point he is still without sin, he nevertheless is only natural since he has not received the holy life of God. The purpose of God is for Adam to choose the fruit of the tree of life with his own volition so that he might be related to God in divine life. And thus Adam would move from simply being created by God to his being born of Him as well.[4]

Adam's aloneness was "not good." There was a problem in paradise and God purposed to resolve it. Help was on the way—help suitable for the need. For Adam, God created Eve.

The appearance of the woman created the most fundamental relationship known to mankind. He also instituted the same principles for unity that work in every other relationship. By examining God's plan for male/female interaction, we will see principles of God's Master Plan that illustrate how Jew and Gentile can live in unity as One New Man. A remarkable number of parallels apply.

Multiplication by Division

When God created Adam, He made him in the full image of Himself. But when God took the woman from the side of the man, what happened to that image of God? Was it added to? Was it subtracted from? It was neither. It was divided.

God solved the problem of Adam's separateness by dividing. And now, for the image of God to be seen and felt and known and heard and observed in the earth, it must come through both the man and the woman. As they stood together in the garden, this was a picture of the Church to come. Male and female together comprised the structure through which God chose to begin to reveal Himself and make Himself known in the earth. It could never come through men alone; it could never come through women alone. It has to be expressed through the two of them together.

From the beginning of the world, God has shown us what dominion would look like. Adam and Eve became "one flesh," yet maintained their individual identities. God took from Adam's side a bride, the foreshadowing of another bride that was yet to come. Eve was like Adam in terms of her humanity, but radically different from him in other ways. God had fashioned her and made her what she needed to be to walk with Adam as his other self—his counterpart. She was God's idea, and together they were God's design for the fulfillment of His plan of subduing the earth and taking dominion over it. God called her a help that was "meet," meaning "suitable" and adequate for him, one who could come alongside him and walk with him in a deeply purposeful way.

The first parallel, then, that we should note is that being One New Man does not mean that Jew and Gentile must become something that they are not. The differences between us were part of God's design, so that each could bring something of value to the relationship. God chose Israel as His people in order to bring reconciliation to the entire world. Gentiles have unique characteristics purposefully intended to provide suitable or adequate help. They are to help each other.

Divine Help, Human Help

What does "help" look like? Again, by looking at God's design for the first man and woman, we see a picture of God's Master Plan. The Hebrew word for help, *ezer*, means "to surround, to protect, to aid, succor." Webster's definition of *succor* is "help, to run under, to give aid or assistance in time of distress." *Help* or *ezer* is an extremely strong word, used 21 times in Scripture. Sixteen times it refers to divine help (God Himself) and five times to human help, but always in the context of help in time of trouble or help against one's enemies. The use of the word itself reveals God's intent in sending Adam a help. God had fashioned the woman in such a unique way that she would be used to surround and protect Adam.

God didn't send Adam a fishing buddy or a coach. He sent him a woman because then, as now, it is the woman who is uniquely crafted by God to touch his heart, to engage his heart, and to help him open his heart to her and to God.

Eve represents both human and divine help in that she was fashioned and sent from the hand of God. The emphasis was on the divine quality of the help she brought to Adam. In Psalm 121:1-2, the word *help* reflects this definition: *"I will lift up my eyes to the hills—from whence comes my help? My help comes from the LORD, Who made heaven and earth."*

She is not the man's savior, but she can be used to open and engage his heart in relationship at a deeper level, hence, bringing him out of his aloneness. She will also complete him in their role as dominion takers—those who move in divine displacement of God's enemy, satan. She was fashioned by the Father's hand and sent from His heart into a situation that needed help.

What would happen if Gentiles, instead of seeing themselves as replacements for Israel, began to think in terms of being a suitable help, grafted into Israel to "surround, to protect, to aid, to succor" God's chosen people? Could that be what Paul had in mind when he told the Romans that Israel had not stumbled beyond recovery (see Rom. 11:11)?

> *I am talking to you Gentiles. Inasmuch as I am the apostle to the Gentiles, I make much of my ministry in the hope that I may somehow arouse my own people to envy and save some of them* (Romans 11:13-14 NIV).

Paul, the Jew, was an apostle to the Gentiles, bringing the good news of the Jewish Messiah to them, looking to them for help in the reconciliation of Israel to God. Paul understood the importance of each part of the body of Messiah bringing its own unique gift into the relationship for the whole to be healthy. Each has been given grace, *"as Messiah apportioned it"* (Eph. 4:7 NIV).

> *From Him the whole body, joined and held together by every supporting ligament, grows and builds itself up in love, as each part does its work* (Ephesians 4:16 NIV).

Side by Side

Equality and Unity are inherent in the biblical description of the creation of woman:

God caused a deep sleep to fall on Adam, and he slept; and He took one of his ribs, and closed up the flesh in its place. Then the rib which the LORD God had taken from man He made into a woman, and He brought her to the man (Genesis 2:21-22).

Eve was not fashioned from a place under Adam's foot; nor was she taken from his shoulder, his elbow, his hip, or some other part of his body. She was drawn from his side because she was created to walk side by side with him. She was crafted to come forth and walk side by side with him in a meaningful, powerful, authoritative way, so the two of them together would be fruitful, be blessed, and walk in dominion in the earth.

Eve's creation from the side of Adam teaches us that she was part of him, an extension of himself. When she was created, part of him was removed and returned to him in a very different package. The woman was not formed of new elements; she was not taken from the dust, hence, separate or independent from the man in that sense. She was part of who he was. He understood this, and delighted in it, saying, *"This is now bone of my bones and flesh of my flesh; she shall be called Woman, because she was taken out of Man"* (Gen. 2:23).

Adam identified with Eve, recognizing the vital part she played in fulfilling his own purpose. Different as they were in so many ways, they were one in purpose. So closely were they joined that Adam could easily envision them as one flesh, as one person.

"Bone of my bones and flesh of my flesh" is an apt illustration of God's idea of unity. Paul's description of the One New Man expresses the same idea in slightly different words, but still with the idea of a unified body:

This mystery is that through the gospel the Gentiles are heirs together with Israel, members together of one body, and sharers together in the promise in Messiah Yeshua (Ephesians 3:6 NIV).

The Church was Jewish at its inception. The first Gentile believers did not start a separate, Gentile Church. They joined in fellowship with Jewish brothers and sisters. They were one. They supported each other, prayed for each other, encouraged one another and helped one another, just as they would in a healthy marriage.

As the Gospel spread, the number of Gentiles in the Church grew proportionately, until the Church was more Gentile than Jewish. In a very real sense, the Gentile church was created from the "side" of the Jewish church. And the relationship between the two grew out of that division in much the same way. Just as Adam and Eve stood side by side, jointly fulfilling God's purpose, each contributing unique strength and vitality to the process, so Jew and Gentile arc called to stand side by side.

His intent was that now, through the church, the manifold wisdom of God should be made known to the rulers and authorities in the heavenly realms, according to his eternal purpose which he accomplished in Christ Jesus our Lord (Ephesians 3:10-11 NIV).

Understanding God's Original Design

The One New Man was created to declare God's wisdom. The second half of Ephesians expands that idea, explaining the practical ways in which we do that. We are called to maturity, which leads to growth and to the exercise of our dominion. We are challenged to *"make every effort to keep the unity of the Spirit through the bond of peace"* (see Eph. 4:3). The goal is to *"prepare God's people for works of service, so that the body of Messiah may be built up"* (see Eph. 4:12).

What exactly is God's original design? The Master Plan is for unity. Growth and dominion are ambitious goals that no one can accomplish alone. It takes the joint effort of the whole body of Messiah, Jew and Gentile, male and female. Unity is essential, and always has been. He clearly revealed His plan and intention in Adam and Eve. It is worth looking at it because it is still God's intention for His people. It is further exemplified in His intention for the One New Man:

> So God created man in His own image; in the image of God He created him; male and female He created them. Then God blessed them, and God said to them, "Be fruitful and multiply; fill the earth and subdue it; have dominion over the fish of the sea, over the birds of the air, and over every living thing that moves on the earth" (Genesis 1:27-28).

From these verses, we can see that male and female were originally designed and created to express God's image on earth. They were to be fruitful, multiply, subdue the earth, and take dominion over it. Through them God intended to manifest Himself—His nature, His character, and His authority, displaying His indisputable power over the works of darkness, thus subduing His archenemy, satan.

What Does This Mean?

The idea of "being fruitful and multiplying" is often applied strictly to the realm of marriage and family; while it does apply, it goes far beyond physical reproduction. To *multiply* means "to be in authority, to enlarge, to increase." This is growth. It is about the increase and multiplication of God's life and authority in us, individually and corporately—and it is about the will of heaven being brought forth on earth.

Note that God blessed the man and the woman. The meaning of the word *bless* extends far beyond our modern-day usage of it.

The fact that God blessed them does not simply mean He wanted them to be happy and fulfilled and to enjoy their lives together. God was setting His structure in place, declaring His purpose, and revealing His heart intent toward mankind.

The word *blessing* means: "increase, faithfulness, multiplication" and "prosperity." God spoke this word of blessing over the male and female. Through these two, Adam and Eve, God's intention was to establish His Kingdom on earth—to bring heaven to earth, to reveal Himself, and to make Himself known in the earth.

Blessing also means victory over our enemies. Establishing His Kingdom meant challenging the dominion of Satan. Adam and Eve became the front line of that battle. The blessing of God enabled them to walk in victory over their enemies, subduing and taking dominion over every foe that would arise against God's revealed plan. This is thread that runs throughout the Word of God. It was set in place from the beginning.

Look at the words *subdue* and *dominion*. The word *subdue* means: to conquer, tread down, force, keep under, and bring into subjection. The word *dominion* means: to prevail against, to take or to rule over.

Clearly, mankind was made to walk in authority. This was the word given to God's first "image bearers," the man and woman together. Satan had already fallen like lightning from heaven (see Luke 10:18). This was the enemy they were instructed to guard against, to subdue. Satan was the one who had boldly declared that he intended to *"exalt [his] throne above the stars of God"* and *"be like the Most High"* (Isa. 14:13-14). God had already declared war on His enemy. Satan's rebellion was to be dealt with. God would use mere humans to subdue the one who had formerly officiated in the heavenly realms.

Declaring War

From the time Lucifer rose up against God, declaring his intent to exalt himself above God, God's response was swift and very direct:

> *How you are fallen from heaven, O Lucifer, son of the morning! How you are cut down to the ground, you who weakened the nations! . . . Those who see you will gaze at you, and consider you, saying: "Is this the man who made the earth tremble, who shook kingdoms, who made the world as a wilderness and destroyed its cities, who did not open the house of his prisoners?" ... The LORD of hosts has sworn, saying, "Surely, as I have thought, so it shall come to pass, and as I have purposed, so it shall stand: that I will break the Assyrian [a type of anti-Messiah spirit] in My land, and on My mountains tread him underfoot"... For the LORD of hosts has purposed, and who will annul it? His hand is stretched out, and who will turn it back?* (Isa. 14:12,16-17,24-27).

God had declared war on His enemy. Satan would be trodden underfoot. The eyes of God's people were to be opened to who he really is: the one who made the world a wilderness and brought destruction to its cities. The earth had been made for humanity to rule over on God's behalf and God would use mankind to overcome His enemy. In response, Satan attempted to put his enemies at enmity with each other—male against female, Gentile against Jew.

An Attempt to Undermine God's Plan

I do not think it was happenstance that the enemy approached the woman first in the garden. He who led the rebellion in heaven now seeks to continue it on earth. He was after the plan of God. He wanted to exalt himself above the Most High God.

Satan was present when the words of God were spoken forth in the garden. He heard God say that man's aloneness was not good. He knew that God had fashioned a "help" suitable for man—a help who would walk with him and, most importantly, be the expression of dominion in the earth with him that God had intended. He knew that she had a highly significant place in man's life and in God's plan.

In approaching the woman first in the garden, perhaps Satan knew that in order to disrupt the plan of God, his best strategy would be to *attack the help God sent*. Satan ultimately purposed to silence the woman, to render her useless and powerless in the man's life, but further, to so weaken her in God's ultimate plan that the whole plan would be ineffectual.

One only has to look at the breakdown of the family structure and society, the growing rejection of long-accepted morals and standards, and the war against the definition of marriage as a union between a man and a woman to realize that we are in a spiritual war beyond anything the Church could have imagined in past times. The liberal press, the gay agenda, and the rise of Islam in the world are not just threats to Christianity, but also strikes against God Himself. They represent an anti-Messiah spirit that is coming against the very plan of God, the very structure He set in place from the beginning—that of the union, the strength, the dominion God intended for the man and woman.

It is not coincidental, either, that anti-Semitism has been so prevalent throughout history. Satan has attempted to eliminate the very existence of Jews for the same reason he has attacked women. He seeks to disrupt the plan of God. The prophets of Israel declared over and over that the redeemer of mankind, the one who would bring reconciliation to the world, would not only come through a woman, He would come specifically through a Jewish woman.

Satan's efforts to destroy Israel have been unsuccessful in spite of centuries of hatred and overt genocide. Unable to carry out that plan, he has sought to keep Jews and Gentiles separated. Just as he saw the importance of Eve to God's purpose for Adam, he recognized that Jews and Gentiles standing together in unity to fulfill God's plan would utterly destroy him. He has done and will continue to do everything he can to keep Jew and Gentile apart. No wonder he has made things difficult for Israel.

The Church must see what is taking place and begin to move into a greater place of authority, but that cannot happen without the Church first seeing the strength of the place of those whom Satan seeks to separate. This includes the woman and the help she was designed to be not only in a marriage union, but also as a voice within the Church, the family, and society. It also includes the diversity represented by both Jew and Gentile. It is the hour for the Church to awaken and arise to its fullest capacity and take dominion.

Exposed!

God's purpose in this world requires unity, oneness, and rec-onciliation. Satan, in opposition to that plan, has sought from the beginning to disrupt unity in every way that he can. He deter-mined to create separateness and division anywhere that God wanted oneness. At the most foundational level, his attack has been focused on the helper God created to surround the heart of man.

I said earlier that the principles involved in this issue of unity were the same, regardless of the nature of the wall of separation. Satan's opposition to the unity between Jew and Gentile stems from the same motivation and creates many of the same problems for mankind. Note some of the similarities.

God's plan for the original union of man and woman was for them to have dominion over the earth and to "multiply," that is, to enlarge and increase. God *blessed* them for the purpose of fulfilling His plan.

In much the same way, Israel was chosen to be the firstfruits of humanity, in order that they might become a blessing to the Gentiles. Unity between the two would fully establish God's dominion, His kingdom, on the earth.

It was not good for man to be alone, or specifically, to be separated. Neither was it good for Israel to be alone and separated. As Eve was a helper for Adam, designed to "surround, to protect, to aid, to succor," God intended that Gentile believers should do the same for Israel, assisting and partnering in the mission of establishing the kingdom of God. Israel was designed to give birth to and to nurture the Messianic hope of the world. Just as Adam and Eve were created to fulfill specific roles in God's Master Plan for the family, so Jew and Gentile were designed to play key parts in His plan for the earth and for mankind.

Just as it was not happenstance that Satan attacked Eve first, his desire to eliminate Jews from the earth is intentional. Genesis 3 reveals the reason for the ongoing abuse and suppression of women throughout history and to this day. Following the tragic events of the Fall, God came in the cool of the evening, and in response to God's questions, Eve responded, *"The serpent deceived me, and I ate"* (Gen. 3:13e). It was the woman who first exposed the enemy for who he really is—the deceiver. She had exposed God's enemy and God spoke into that, in essence saying, "Now forever and ever, Satan, down through the centuries she will be used again and again to expose you and to call you who you really are!"

Further, God declared that the woman would be instrumental in Satan's ultimate demise. Scripture states it this way:

The LORD said to the serpent... "And I will put enmity between you and the woman, and between your seed and her Seed; He shall bruise your head, and you shall bruise His heel" (Genesis 3:15).

Satan's particular hatred of women comes from his understanding that the Seed of woman would crush him.

Satan's hatred of Israel is based on the same type of understanding. He knew that the Messiah, the Savior of the world, would come through the Jews. Just as he has attacked women throughout history, attempting to silence and incapacitate them, he has sought the marginalization and the destruction of Israel, hoping to disrupt God's ultimate Master Plan. That plan is a covenant that God made with Israel, and God will never break His covenant.

Who's Whose Enemy?

We often refer to satan as our enemy, but in a very real way the exact opposite is true. *We* are *his* enemy! He has known this truth from the beginning, for God stated it directly to him in relation to the woman.

Eve was the first to be ensnared by satan and the first to expose his true nature. She was also the subject of the first promise of deliverance:

When the fullness of the time was come, God sent forth his Son, made of a woman, made under the law, to redeem them that were under the law, that we might receive the adoption as sons (Galatians 4:4-5 KJV).

Through the Seed of the woman, *"[sin and] death [would be] swallowed up in victory"* (1 Cor. 15:54). Through the Seed of the woman, God would *"[disarm] principalities and powers, [making] a public spectacle of them, triumphing over them in it"* (Col. 2:15). Heaven and earth's greatest victory would be realized out of the greatest point of defeat.

Note in this verse that the fullness of time has also revealed the close connection between man and woman, and Jew and Gentile. God sent forth His Son as a man, born of woman, under the Torah, as a Jew, to redeem the Jews and to make possible the adoption as sons of Gentiles.

The unity of Jew and Gentile is an absolutely essential element in God's plan. They are different, yet God desired them to stand together in unity. The One New Man transcends the differences between the two, joining their individual strengths for establishing the Kingdom of God. Walking together in the power and love of God, nothing can stop them from fulfilling God's purpose.

Separation results in loss. When the Jew becomes so proud of his heritage as God's chosen that he holds the Gentile at a distance, he will never be able to benefit from the support, encouragement, and strength Gentile believers have to offer. When a Gentile believer thinks of himself as Israel's replacement, he will never be able to surround, protect, aid, and succor Israel in establishing God's dominion. Instead they will remain separate, alone. And alone is not good.

To achieve the unity God wants, it is equally essential that we learn to live in unity at the most foundational level of human existence. It will be difficult, if not impossible, for Jew and Gentile to learn mutual respect and cooperation if they do not fully practice respect and cooperation at the basic level of gender relations. This is part of the reason for the passion I feel about the position of women in the Church and in society.

That They May Be One

Yeshua prayed: *"…that they all may be one, as You, Father, are in Me, and I in You; that they also may be one in Us, that the world may believe that You sent Me* (John 17:21).

As we move toward the culmination of the age, just as God used a man and a woman to usher in His first coming, so God will bring the genders together, as well as Jew and Gentile, as one new humanity to prepare the way for His Second Coming.

We, as His body, are being reconciled, one to another: male and female, and Jew and Gentile, so that "the world may believe;" so that the body of Messiah may manifest His glory; so that we may walk in His authority, subduing and taking dominion in the earth and fulfilling the mandate God has given us as His people. The reconciled, reunified body of Messiah is truly the "One New Man."

Bibliography

1001 Quotes, Illustrations, and Humorous Stories for Preachers, Teachers and Writers (2008). Messiahianity Today Intl.

Barnhouse, D. G. (1965). *The Invisible War*. Grand Rapids, MI: Zondervan Publishing House.

Berry, G. R. (1975). *The Interlinear Literal Translation of the Hebrew Old Testament*. Grand Rapids, MI: Kregel Publications.

Nee, W. (1980). *Watchman Nee, Messenger of the Cross*. New York: Messiahian Fellowship Publishers.

The New Unger's Bible Dictionary. (1988). Chicago, Illinois: Originally published by Moody Press.

Endnotes

1. *1001 Quotes, Illustrations, and Humorous Stories for Preachers, Teachers and Writers,* (Messiahianity Today Intl., 2008).

2. *The New Unger's Bible Dictionary.* (Chicago, Illinois: Moody Press. 1988).

3. G.R. Berry, *The Interlinear Literal Translation of the Hebrew Old Testament,* (Grand Rapids, MI: Kregel Publications, 1975).

4. Watchman Nee, *Watchman Nee, Messenger of the Cross.* (New York: Messiahian Fellowship Publishers, 1980) 136-137.

CHAPTER 9

Israel and the Tsunami of World Revival

Peter Tsukahira, Or HaCarmel, Director

I am an Asian-American-Israeli. By that I mean I have an Asian face, an American way of speaking, and an Israeli passport. My grandparents were immigrants to the United States from Japan over 100 years ago. They settled in southern California but were not allowed to have American citizenship until decades later. My parents were born as children of these immigrants and grew up as U.S. citizens. Following the Japanese attack on Pearl Harbor, over 100,000 Americans of Japanese descent, including many of my relatives, were relocated from the West Coast to internment camps hundreds of miles away in the desert for the duration of the war. They lost property, careers, and most importantly, their freedom. This was a shameful chapter in American history that, years later, President Clinton, writing in a personal letter to all Japanese-Americans who had been interned, said was based on "prejudice, war hysteria, and a failure of political leadership."

In the years immediately following the war, Americans were still dealing with its aftermath and the divisions it had created. In the late 1940s, my parents moved to Cambridge, Massachusetts, where I was born and where my father earned his Ph.D. in Asian history at Harvard University. He taught there and at UC Berkeley before deciding to pursue a career with the U.S. Department of State.

We relocated outside Washington, D.C., and again experienced anti-Asian sentiment, as there were neighborhoods in the 1950s that did not welcome people of Asian descent. Ironically, the neighborhood where my family finally bought a home had a majority of Jewish families, since they also felt similarly excluded. In 1960, my father was assigned to the American embassy in Tokyo. So, when I was ten we moved as a family to Japan, which was still in the process of rebuilding after the devastation of World War II. In those days, "made in Japan" meant cheap, low-quality imitations. It was an incredible experience to witness the unfolding of what the world would later see as Japan's "economic miracle."

When I finished high school, I went back to the Boston area for university. There at Tufts University, I met and later married a Jewish woman from New York named Rita. We met in 1969 and were thrown together during the chaotic and sometimes violent era known as America's countercultural revolution. In 1973, the loss of my best friend to suicide drove me out of Boston to New Mexico in search of a new identity. Rita joined me there, and was picked up while hitchhiking and invited to a coffeehouse ministry in Santa Fe called "Shalom." It was at "Shalom" that she heard the Gospel for the first time from another Jewish former hippie and commune founder, Eitan Shishkoff. Within a few weeks, we both committed our lives to the Messiah of Israel and were married soon after. In response to God's call to ministry, we attended a Bible school in Dallas, Texas, and then a seminary in southern California. Integral to our call was a clear sense that we were to eventually serve Him in the land of Israel.

During my years in seminary, I had difficulty paying our expenses, and through a friend found a job in a mini-computer company as a programmer and later in marketing. This job experience provided a vehicle for us to move to Japan in the early 1980s. Rita taught communication at a local university and I worked in the burgeoning Japanese computer industry while helping to establish and lead an international congregation in Tokyo. In December 1987, the doors opened for us to immigrate to Israel. We arrived directly from Japan the day after the start of the first *intifada,* or Palestinian uprising. Israel's ongoing conflict with the Palestinians has had a defining influence on our lives in Israel over the past more than 20 years.

What has it been like for a person like me with Asian ancestry to become an Israeli and then a leader in the embryonic and emerging Israeli Messianic community? Well, to be sure, God has allowed me to be stretched spiritually and molded like clay for His unique purposes. I sometimes say that the difference culturally between Japan and Israel is like the difference between silk and sandpaper! This is not a value judgment—each has its own particular use and one cannot be substituted for the other.

Our two children have grown up in Israel. Our daughter was two when we moved from Japan and our son was born on Mt. Carmel. In one sense, I am repeating the new immigrant experience of my grandparents—however, in a completely different context. Spiritually, it could be said the following Scripture applies to me:

> *"So you shall divide this land among yourselves according to the tribes of Israel. You shall divide it by lot for an inheritance among yourselves and among the aliens who stay in your midst, who bring forth sons in your midst. And they shall be to you as the native-born among the sons of Israel; they shall be allotted an inheritance with you among the tribes of Israel. And in the tribe with which the alien stays, there you shall give him his inheritance,"* declares the Lord GOD (Ezekiel 47:21-23 NASB).

My life has been lived between three very different cultures. As a Japanese-American, my early years were spent as a bridge between East and West. Later, as an Israeli immigrant, I accepted an even greater challenge. Nevertheless, I have found my new homeland to be rich beyond description in truth about God and the Bible. As a Gentile, "grafted" into the Abrahamic tree by faith, I have discovered and received an abundant inheritance here in this land.

In 1991, just after the end of the first Gulf War, we joined with another couple, David and Karen Davis, who, like ourselves, were new immigrants, a Jew and a Gentile called together for God's purposes. They were pioneering a rehabilitation center for Jewish and Arab men in our city. We began praying together and soon felt God was calling us to begin a new congregation in our city. From the start, this ministry was built on the foundational value of the "One New Man" as found in Ephesians 2:15. That is Jew and Gentile together as a dwelling place for God in the Spirit. Over the years, we have been privileged to participate in the planting of several other Hebrew and Arabic-speaking congregations. All of our own ministries, including the shelter for women started by Rita in 2003, are focused on serving both Jews and non-Jews with the same love of God.

God's original calling for the Jewish people was to be blessing to the rest of the world. When God called Abram to be the special instrument of His will, He made it clear there was divine purpose behind the offer of covenantal friendship. God said:

> *And I will bless those who bless you, and the one who curses you I will curse.* ***And in you all the families of the earth will be blessed*** (Genesis 12:3 NASB).

This is reiterated in the prophets when Isaiah wrote concerning God's servant, Israel:

*He says, "It is too small a thing that You should be My Servant to raise up the tribes of Jacob and to restore the preserved ones of Israel; **I will also make You a light of the nations** So that My salvation may reach to the end of the earth"* (Isaiah 49:6 NASB).

Again in the New Testament, when Jesus preached in His own hometown of Nazareth, according to Luke's account in chapter 4, the initial Messianic proclamation He made was greeted with approval. Then He reminded the Jews gathered in the synagogue that the prophet Elijah was sent to help a Syrophoenician (Lebanese) widow and his disciple, Elisha, healed only a Syrian general of leprosy. Sadly, the latter part of Jesus' message was met with hostility. Despising their calling to bless the Gentiles, the people of Nazareth wanted to kill their town's most famous son.

The apostle Paul makes the point in Romans 11:29 that the *"gifts and calling of God are irrevocable"* (NASB). In context, the inspired writer is applying this truth specifically to Israel, in spite of her disobedience. We Gentiles may "borrow" this verse for other uses as the Holy Spirit leads, but when we are finished using it, we should return it where it was found! What are the "gifts" God has given Israel if they do not include the land to be a nation, and what is the "calling" if not to serve as a priestly kingdom (see Exod. 19:6) and to take God's message to the rest of the world?

As Rita and I traveled from the United States to Japan and then to Israel, I began to see a majestic end-time convergence between God's plan for Israel and His plan for the nations. The "Bride" that will welcome the Messiah's return will be a "One New Man" company made of all nations, tribes, and tongues. Of course, His Bride can never be complete without the Jewish people. Paul wrote in Romans 11:25-26 that Israel's salvation is not independent from revival in the nations:

*For I do not want you, brethren, to be uninformed of this mystery—so that you will not be wise in your own estimation— that **a partial hardening has happened to Israel until the fullness of the Gentiles has come in; and so all Israel will be saved**; just as it is written, "The Deliverer will come from Zion, He will remove ungodliness from Jacob"* (NASB).

As both Israel and the nations rise to the fulfillment of their respective callings, we will begin to see the completion of God's end-time purposes. At the end of Matthew's Gospel, Jesus personally predicted two great prophetic fulfillments that must take place before His return. The first is found at the end of Matthew 23. He said:

*Jerusalem, Jerusalem, who kills the prophets and stones those who are sent to her! How often I wanted to gather your children together, the way a hen gathers her chicks under her wings, and you were unwilling. Behold, your house is being left to you desolate! For I say to you, from now on you will not see Me until you say, **"Blessed is He Who comes in the name of the Lord!"*** (Matthew 23:37-39 NASB)

Jesus' words mean there must be a Messianic Jerusalem that will welcome Him back as Messiah and King. Today, we sing that last verse in Hebrew, *"Baruch haba bashem Adonai,"* as an intercessory prayer on behalf of unbelieving Jerusalem. A Messianic congregational leader who came to faith in the 1960s told me that at that time he knew of only five other believers in Jerusalem. Now we estimate there are between 10,000 and 15,000 Israeli Messianic believers in the country, and many of them are living and worshipping in Jerusalem. Progress is being made toward the fulfillment of Jesus' first prediction.

The second end-time prediction Jesus made is found in Matthew 24. In response to a direct question about the end times from

His own disciples, after giving a list of signs that describe our day with uncanny accuracy, Jesus said this:

> This **gospel of the kingdom** *shall be preached in the whole world as a testimony to all the nations, and then the end will come* (Matthew 24:14 NASB).

Here, again, we see the dual emphasis in the "One New Man" expressed as Israel *together with* the nations in God's plan for the world. Jerusalem must be saved and welcome Jesus back as King. At the same time, all nations must experience revival through the Gospel of the Kingdom. Because of the modern "resurrection" of the nation of Israel and the re-emergence of Messianic Jews after 2,000 years of a primarily Gentile church, we are the first generation to see the coming fulfillment of the "One New Man" with our own eyes!

The Gospel of the Kingdom is more than a message of salvation. The Kingdom of God that Jesus preached was rooted deeply in the identity of Israel as a nation. Jews know that God became King of Israel in the desert after the exodus from Egyptian slavery. Jews also know that God ruled Israel with laws that extended to every area of society and culture. The Gospel of the Kingdom therefore is a nation-forming, culture-transforming message. It is revival that reforms.

In the early years of Christian history, the Gospel moved powerfully out of Israel into the Gentile world. Paul's Macedonian vision in Acts 16 made it clear that God's strategic direction for the Gospel of the kingdom was west. Even though initially the message of the New Testament went out in all directions, the record of where it took root and transformed culture shows the Gospel of the Kingdom always moved to the west even until today.

During Paul's lifetime, the Gospel saturated the Greek-speaking world. Our earliest New Testaments are written in Greek and contain letters to Greek cities like Philippi, Corinth, and

Thessalonica. Paul preached on Mars Hill in Athens to the philosophers there. Then the Gospel message continued west, following the roads that, according to the saying, all led to Rome. There the Gospel of the Kingdom fought a life and death struggle with the Roman imperial system for more than two hundred years. Early Christians became identified as enemies of the state. At various times they were cruelly persecuted and brutally martyred. Still the followers of Jesus' Gospel persisted and eventually they outlasted the mighty Roman Empire.

Rome became increasingly corrupt and collapsed. Barbarians from the north sacked the great empire. Who were these semi-civilized, pagan tribesmen? *"You will be hearing of wars and rumors of wars. See that you are not frightened, for those things must take place, but that is not yet the end"* (Matt. 24:6 NASB).

The barbarians that sacked Rome were called Goths, Visigoths, Vandals, and the Huns. History shows that they were gradually transformed by the Christian faith. Pagan tribesmen were the ancestors of the very civilized Swiss, Dutch, French, British, and Germans of today. The miracle of Christian Europe is that local people and their leaders began to believe a Gospel that was at first totally foreign to them. Christianity moved like a tidal wave across the continent, transforming whole nations and sinking down into the roots of European culture.

The story of how a mighty Christian civilization arose in Europe is too complex for one person to tell, but in general, the Gospel of the Kingdom provided Europe with a foundation of truth that many built upon. Artists and scientists, scholars, merchants, and lawmakers discovered, created, and governed in ways that over time resulted in unprecedented knowledge, wealth, influence, and power.

Eventually, the accomplishments of European nations began to tower over the rest of the world. Europeans navigated the globe and became dominant politically and militarily. Were European people smarter than everyone else? Did they work harder? This cannot be true. Chinese scientists invented gunpowder and printing centuries before they were known in Europe. The Arabs were more advanced in mathematics. Why did Europe prosper so spectacularly and become so dominant? The answer must be that in Acts chapter 16, the apostle Paul, an Asian Jew by birth, saw a European Gentile in his Macedonian vision and took the Gospel of the Kingdom west.

Actually, Paul surely understood God's strategic direction for the Gospel by the end of his apostolic ministry. In the fifteenth chapter of his letter to the Romans, Paul wrote twice that he intended to come to Rome on his way to Spain. Fourteen hundred years before Columbus discovered America, Spain was the "end of the world" and as far west as anyone could go in Paul's day.

Wherever European Christians went throughout the world, they also took the Gospel message. The seeds of faith were planted by missionaries, both Catholic and Protestant, in every continent. Eventually, however, in Europe, Christian culture became too dominant. New Protestant movements like the early Baptists, Quakers, Mennonites, Huguenots, and Puritans found no freedom to worship God as they understood Him from the Bible. Some of them called themselves "pilgrims" and looked for a new world to find freedom. They decided to leave Europe and went west across the great Atlantic.

In 1620, a small ship called the *Mayflower* sailed from Plymouth, England, with 102 pilgrims and settlers bound for America. They landed in what later was called Massachusetts and within one year, half had died. Still, in the years that followed an increasing number of pilgrims continued to arrive in the New World. What motivated them to accept such risk and harsh conditions? A vision of a "new Jerusalem," that is, a new nation built on Christian principles that would guarantee the freedom of every individual to worship God according to the Bible.

In a relatively short period of time, historically speaking, the United States emerged as a powerful nation, bursting with creativity and vitality, with "liberty and justice for all." Soon American achievements in science, industry, agriculture, law, and business management made it tower over all that had been previously accomplished in Europe. Were North Americans more intelligent than everyone else in the world? Did they work harder? The key to American greatness lies in the fact that the apostle Paul took the Gospel west in Acts chapter 16 and that the United States was established on a godly, biblical base by the Founding Fathers.

During the last hundred years, the Gospel has moved powerfully in Latin America and Africa, sweeping millions into the Kingdom. Great change is taking place around the world, but nowhere more significantly than west from America, across the Pacific Ocean, in East Asia. Presbyterianism traces its roots to Scotland and the ministry of John Knox nearly 500 years ago, but today the largest, most vibrant Presbyterian churches are found in Korea. Methodism began almost 300 years ago in England, but today the largest and most rapidly growing Methodist churches are found in Korea. Pentecostalism began in the United States 100 years ago, but today the greatest Pentecostal church, which is also the largest single congregation in history (weekly attendance close to 800,000), is the Yoido Full Gospel Church in Seoul, Korea. When did Korean Christianity reach such massive proportions? Only in the last 50 years. Dr. David Yonggi Cho began the Yoido Full Gospel Church with five members in 1958.

The wave of transformation through the Gospel of the Kingdom predicted by Jesus 2,000 years ago is still moving westward, but it is moving faster now, and the wave is much larger. It is a veritable tsunami of revival and reform. The modern Christian revival in Korea is only surpassed by what has taken place during the same time period in China. Now it is estimated that there are 135 million Christians in Mainland China, about 10 percent of the total population and almost double the size of the Chinese Communist Party. Visitors to churches in China often comment on the passion and commitment of the Chinese Christians in the face of ongoing persecution. What massive changes lie ahead for this region?

The leading edge of this westward sweeping tidal wave of spiritual transformation is defined by the fact that in Asia today, almost all the Christians are first-generation believers. As Asian Christians mature spiritually, they are growing in the revelation of God's faithfulness to His original covenant people, the Jews. There is also an increasing desire to reach out as brothers in the Lord to Messianic believers in Israel. Moving west from Korea and the Chinese coastal regions, the Gospel of the Kingdom is now impacting India and Southeast Asia with unprecedented and amazing force. The recent surge in numbers of new believers in this generation alone is nothing short of breathtaking. Today, some of the largest church buildings in the world are being planned or under construction in India and Indonesia (the world's most populous Muslim nation). At the same time, the economic power of Asian countries, especially China, is beginning to be felt around the world.

Where is this giant wave of revival and transformation heading? Westward, across Central Asia, through the "back door" of the Islamic world and back to Jerusalem, where it all began. If you look west along the ancient "Silk Road" from India, you see Pakistan, Afghanistan, Iran, Iraq, Syria, and Lebanon. Each of these countries is now in the awful grip of "wars and rumors of wars," just as Jesus predicted to His disciples in Matthew 24. We should not overlook the fact that in both Korea and China, war and social upheaval immediately preceded massive transforming revival. Jesus said,

The time has come to awaken the "One New Man" vision that was such an important part of the New Testament writers' world-view. The two great prophetic fulfillments taught by Jesus to His disciples on the Mount of Olives (where He will return) have now become visible for the first time in two thousand years. Through the growth and maturity of Israeli Messianic Jews in the face of deep cultural and spiritual resistance, Jerusalem will eventually say, "Blessed is He who comes in the name of the Lord!" to Yeshua, the Jewish Messiah. This is converging with the "fullness of the Gentiles" coming to faith through the Gospel of the Kingdom in every previously unreached nation. The point of convergence is in Israel and the joining of Jew and Gentile in one body through the shared sacrificial work of Jesus, the Son of God.

As a prophetic and apostolic body, members of the Kingdom everywhere should stand in support of Israeli Messianic Jews and also pray for great end-time revival in the remaining unreached nations—primarily the Islamic world. In our own congregation on Mt. Carmel, Messianic Jews and Arab Christians regularly meet to worship, pray, and serve the Lord together. It has been my privilege over the years to travel both to East Asia and Europe with believing Jews and Arabs to demonstrate our unity in Messiah through conferences and church services. The inspired psalmist wrote, *"Pray for the peace of Jerusalem: May they prosper who love you"* (Ps. 122:6 NASB).

The way to pray for the peace of Jerusalem is to pray that the Prince of Peace will rule in the hearts of Jerusalem's people and that He will bring Jews and Gentiles together as "One New Man," His beloved body, the end-time Bride.

CHAPTER 10

Where Are
All the Jews?

Jonathan Bernis, Jewish Voice, President

Any valid discussion of the *One New Man* must include the understanding that it is a prophetic picture of two distinct groups becoming one in Messiah *spiritually*—Jews and Gentiles together as one. For this glorious reality to be realized in our day, a healthy balance of both must be represented in the Body, each living out their unique culture, identity, and calling.

While I am not advocating a quota or a specific ratio, if there is to be an appropriate balance between Jews and Gentiles in the Body of Believers (it is certainly unlikely that it would be 50/50 since God created so many more Gentiles than Jews), I can say with certainty that there are still far too few Jewish believers to claim that the One New Man has matured. The Church is still essentially Gentile with a small, but growing number of Jewish believers emerging over the last 40 years. Why is this the case, and how can it be changed? How do we see more Jews come into the Kingdom of God?

The answers can be found in the apostle Paul's letter to the church in Rome upon the completion of his third missionary journey. Chapters 9-11 of the book of Romans are the definitive New Testament teaching concerning God's plan for the restoration of Israel (the Jewish people).

Sadly, many Christian teachers today either tend to overlook these critically important chapters altogether, or even worse, spiritualize their meaning and interpret the promises to be redirected to the Church, completely discarding God's faithful promises that He made with the Children of Abraham, Isaac, and Jacob.

As the apostle to the Gentiles, Paul warned them, *"Do not boast against the branches. But if you do boast, remember that you do not support the root, but the root supports you"* (Rom. 11:18). Clearly, the seeds of a most damaging false teaching were already beginning to sprout during Paul's lifetime.

Replacement Theology

Although numerous reasons exist as to why we see so few Jews today who believe in Jesus, I want to focus on two that, without question, have been the most damaging. Ironically, they are at opposite ends of the spectrum. The first can be identified as the ancient *Doctrine of Supersessionism*, or as it is more commonly referred to these days, *replacement theology*.

Originating as early as the mid-second century A.D., replacement theology is a direct plan of the enemy to discard and destroy the very people who were commissioned first to bring God's message of redemption to the World.

It places the blame squarely on the Jews for the death of Christ, unequivocally stating that the Jews' rejection of Jesus as Messiah and their ultimate act of rebellion or disobedience by killing the Son of God, or *deicide,* has resulted in their permanent revocation, and maintains that the Chosen People are now eternally under the judgment of God. This thinking has resulted in the mistaken belief that the Jewish people have been *replaced* by a *Spiritual Israel*— God's new priesthood and holy nation—the Church.

Now most people honestly claim that they have never heard of *replacement theology* or the *doctrine of supersessionism,* and I believe that is true. They haven't been blatantly exposed to the specific terminology. Without realizing it, however, they do hold anti-Jewish or anti-Semitic views. Why? The answer is simple— this false theology is coming from the pulpits of many mainstream denominations.

Erroneous doctrine must be purged from the Church in order for more Jewish people to come into the Kingdom of God!

Replacement theology runs absolutely contrary to the teaching of Scripture and is a demonically inspired lie. Sadly, this lie has resulted in an almost 2,000-year legacy of hatred, persecution, and murder against the Jewish people in the name of Christ and Christianity. The Crusades, the Spanish Inquisition, the pogroms of Eastern Europe, and ultimately the Holocaust were all *justified* by this horrible doctrine and seen as God's retribution against His enemy, the Jews, the murderers of His Son.

I regularly hear statements like, "There's nothing special about the Jewish people," or, "God doesn't love the Jews more than anyone else," or, "Reaching non-Jews is just as important as reaching Jews." Though not entirely untrue, the tone of these statements is usually hostile and is often a reflection of the negative attitudes that have come about through the residue of replacement theology.

Although the view that God hates the Jews and is irrevocably finished with them is too extreme for true Christians to cling to in good conscience, many Christians commonly believe a subtle, yet more dangerous variation. They still assume that the Jews are solely responsible for killing Jesus and, therefore, the Gospel is no longer to the Jew first.

Need we ask why Jews are so negative to the Gospel? To the advocates of replacement theology, Jews today are nothing more than the descendants of those horrible people who killed the Son of God, and deserve to be punished. Having gone so far as to identify themselves as Christians while they carried out their evil deeds, they have given Jews a twisted and corrupt perception of Christianity.

Dual Covenant Theology

At the opposite end of the spectrum to replacement theology, we find another hindrance to the realization of the One New Man in the form of what has come to be known as *Dual Covenant theology*. Simply stated, this position promulgates the idea that the Jewish people have a separate path to salvation through the Abrahamic or Mosaic Covenant. In other words, this view holds that Jews do not need Jesus for personal salvation.

Proponents of this theology teach that both Judaism and Christianity are valid yet distinct religions, each equally worthy of the other's full acceptance and respect. To say it another way, Christians should not challenge traditional Judaism's rejection of Jesus as the Messiah.

Sparked by guilt over the extermination of six million Jews under the guise of Christ and Christianity during the Holocaust, liberal Christian scholars began to write and teach that the Jews had suffered enough through the centuries, and since much of this suffering was due to efforts to try to force Jews to convert to Christianity, we now need to leave them alone. As a result, many Christians, including Evangelicals, consider it an expression of good will and honor to *not* to share the Gospel with Jewish people.

While this may be based on the truth that we should honor Israel, and it can even appear to be noble, the Bible does not declare that the Gospel is for the Jewish people *also*, but the Gospel is to the Jew *first* (see Rom. 1:16). There is only one plan of salvation for all people. Jesus Himself said in John 14:6, *"I am the way, the truth, and the life. No one comes to the Father except through me."* As Bible believers, we have no choice but to accept this at face value. Either you believe God's Word or you don't.

But you don't have to fully espouse "Dual Covenant Theology" to miss the mark. Some Christian Zionist leaders, while not fully embracing a Dual Covenant view, do teach that sharing the Gospel with Jewish people is unnecessary. I recently heard one prominent leader (who I otherwise greatly respect) make the statement, "Jews do not come to Christ through proclamation, but through revelation."

Apparently, this leader feels it is God's job and He will take care of it on His own. And while this is not technically a "dual Covenant" position, the end result is the same—the misguided belief that there is no need to share our faith with Jewish people. The perpetuation of this view would be a tragedy with incalculable ramifications and a direct contradiction of what the Bible clearly teaches about our individual responsibility to help bring about the redemption of Israel.

Paul's Heart Cry for the Salvation of Israel

Paul begins his teaching concerning Israel in Romans 9 with an astounding statement:

I speak the truth in Christ—I am not lying, my conscience confirms it in the Holy Spirit—I have great sorrow and unceasing anguish in my heart. For I could wish that I myself were cursed and cut off from Christ for the sake

of my brothers, those of my own race, the people of Israel
(Romans 9:1-4 NIV).

I've reflected on these verses for many years, and I am astounded every time I read them. Paul is actually taking an oath of sorts, as one would do before testifying in a court of law when a witness places his left hand on the Bible, raises his right hand, and pledges "to speak the whole truth and nothing but the truth so help me God."

Paul is swearing this oath on the Holy Spirit, because he is telling us something so profound—so unimaginable—that despite his great authority and integrity, he wants to make it clear that he is speaking the absolute truth.

What is this profoundly astonishing statement? He tells us that he would be willing to give up his own salvation—his very eternity in the presence of God—for the sake of his own people, the people of Israel.

I believe that many of us could honestly say that we would be willing to give up our lives for our faith, but Paul is going far beyond that in declaring that he'd be willing to sacrifice his own *eternal* life for the sake of his brethren, the people of Israel. I find Paul's statement to be so astonishing for three very important reasons:

First, I would venture to say that Paul understood better than any of us the riches of Heaven and the torments of hell—complete and total darkness and separation from God. Paul has just finished in the preceding verses to teach about the depth of God's love:

For I am convinced that neither death nor life, neither angels nor demons, neither the present nor the future, nor any powers, neither height nor depth, nor anything else in all creation, will be able to separate us from the love of God that is in Christ Jesus our Lord (Romans 8:38-39 NIV).

And yet he says there is *one thing* for which he would be willing to be separated from God, and that one thing is the salvation of his own people—the people of Israel.

Second, Paul's calling was to be an *apostle to the Gentiles.* You would think as such that he would be emphasizing and reaffirming his commitment and burden for them.

Yet, this is not what he does. Rather, he shares with his Gentile spiritual brethren that his burden is not first and foremost for them, but for his natural blood brothers, his countrymen, the people of Israel.

It seems to me that Paul risks alienating the very people God called him to reach by sharing this, the deepest secret of his heart.

The third thing that astounds me about this declaration is that Paul tells us he is willing to sacrifice his own salvation for the very people who have rejected, ostracized, and persecuted him, stoned him, and beaten him with rods! How can Paul say this about these people who have caused him such pain? There is only one answer. *This is the very heart of God for His beloved Israel, the apple of His eye.*

We witness this same expression of God's heart of love and forgiveness in the parable of the prodigal son in Luke 15:11-24. The father (God) is waiting with longing for his wayward son (Israel) to come home, despite the mistakes of his past, so that he might prepare a feast. This remains the heart of God concerning his people Israel to this very day. He longs for them to return to relationship with him, a relationship that comes through His son, Yeshua.

Finally, this confession of Paul begs the question of why would Paul take such a risk to share this deep secret of his heart with the church at Rome? Why would he risk the negative feelings he might invoke?

I believe Paul wants those whom he loves and who love him to share this same burden he carries for his brothers after the flesh, the people of Israel. In other words, Paul shared this in the hope that true believers might somehow embrace this burden and play their part as co-workers with the Lord to bring about the salvation of Israel.

Who Is Israel?

I find when I talk with people that there is some confusion in regard to whom or what *Israel* actually refers. Many interpret Israel to be the little sliver of land along the Mediterranean Sea that is continuously the center of world tension. But, in fact, when Paul talks about Israel, he's not talking about the land, but rather, the people.

When we look carefully at the many references to *Israel* throughout Romans 9-11, we see that Paul's focus is on their salvation. He's not talking about the *land* of Israel, but the *people* of Israel, living both in the land and scattered throughout the nations. Many Christians confuse this and believe that their support should be centered on the *land* of Israel, when, in fact, the heart cry of Paul is for the salvation of the *people* of Israel. I believe this needs to be our focus as well. In fact, the only reason the *land* is called Israel is because it was given to the *people* of Israel as their inheritance.

Many misguided Christians who genuinely love Israel are expressing that love in so many other ways. Many are focused on the Jewish people returning to the land of Israel. This was not Paul's emphasis. His emphasis was on the salvation of the people of Israel. Don't get me wrong, the return of the Jewish people to their land is certainly a fulfillment of Last Days' prophecy, and it is very important, but in the context of this teaching, it is not what Paul was willing to give up his eternity for.

Many Christians tell me how much they love Israel and then go on to list all of the Judaica they have collected to display in their homes. Others speak of how much they love the Jewish people, and in fact, wish they were Jewish. Oftentimes, these people begin to focus great attention on keeping Torah and seeking to be as Jewish as they can. Again, this may be admirable, but there is a fine line between identifying with the Jewish roots of our faith and being a Jewish "wannabe." The glorious picture of the One New Man is not Gentiles becoming Jews, but rather the two embracing each other while maintaining their own unique calling and identity.

Another disturbing reality is that many Christians who love the Jewish people give large amounts of money (several hundred million dollars each year) to Jewish organizations that do not in any way promote the Gospel. On the contrary, some actually use the money, sent by Christians, to prevent the Gospel from going to Jewish people. A portion of these funds end up in the hands of groups that seek to persecute believers in the land of Israel with the hope of stamping out Messianic faith from the land of Israel.

The Jewish People Need the Gospel

It is vitally important for Christians to understand that a biblical approach to loving the Jewish people must include the *proclamation* of the Gospel. I cannot emphasize this enough. Paul makes it very clear in Romans 1:16 that the Gospel is not only relevant *"for the salvation of everyone who believes,"* but is, in fact, *"first for the Jew, and then for the Gentile"* (NIV).

There is only one Gospel and one name under Heaven by which we must be saved, and it is the Person of Yeshua haMashiach, Jesus the Messiah. By necessity, Christian appreciation of Israel must include a commitment to their salvation. Paul was not willing to give up his eternity for Jews to return to Israel or for Christians to live as Jews, but he was willing to give up his eternal life for the salvation of His people. And that must be our heart as well.

I like to say it this way—Genesis 12:3 declares that, *"I [God] will bless those who bless you [my People, the descendants of Abraham]..."* and the greatest blessing that you can give a Jewish Person is the knowledge of his or her Messiah and eternal life.

The Importance of Proclamation

I stated previously that if you claim to love the Jewish people, any expression of this love that fails to proclaim or share the Gospel in some way is misguided. Paul emphasized this when he declared: *"Brethren, my heart's desire and prayer to God for Israel is that they may be saved"* (Rom. 10:1).

You may wonder why I stress so strongly the salvation of the Jewish people? It is because in order to realize the fulfillment of this glorious truth about the One New Man, we must understand that it requires two peoples coming together: Jew and Gentile. The problem is that for the last 1900 years since the end of the first century, the Church has not been made up of Jew and Gentile—it has been almost exclusively of Gentiles.

It is now God's time for the other half of the Man—the Jewish people—to come into the kingdom of God so that we can truly have the One New Man in all his intended fullness—not Gentiles with a few Jews, but an established Jewish *Ecclesia*—a synagogue of committed Jewish believers—within the Body. The only way this can occur is for more Jews to come into the body of Christ.

How will this happen? Paul very clearly answers this for us:

If you confess with your mouth, "Jesus is Lord," and believe in your heart that God raised Him from the dead, you will be saved. For it is with your heart that you believe and are justified, and it is with your mouth that you confess and are saved (Romans 10:9 NIV).

This is a universal truth. This is the way God's Kingdom has always been expanded and how people have come into new life in God. It is applicable for everyone, but in its context, Paul is speaking of the salvation of Israel. This is how Jewish people as well as Gentiles are born from above. All must believe and confess. This is how Israel will be saved. This is how we will come into the fullness of the One New Man.

Let me say again that this is talking about Israel. Indeed, this is a universal truth, but in its context, it is speaking of God's intended salvation of Israel.

So What's the Problem?

Paul reveals a simple truth to us when he declares *"All who call upon the name of the Lord shall be saved."* It's really that simple. So then, why aren't there more Jewish people saved today?

The answer lies in the verses that follow shortly thereafter:

How then shall they call on Him in whom they have not believed? And how shall they believe in Him of whom they have not heard? And how shall they hear without a preacher? And how shall they preach unless they are sent? (Romans 10:14-15)

This is the crux of the challenge we are facing. Not enough Jewish people are hearing the Gospel. Nor will they hear unless someone proclaims. And that "someone" needs to be you! You see, *proclamation* and *revelation* are not two separate ideas—a person either comes to know the Lord through *proclamation* (hearing) or through *revelation* (a supernatural dream, vision, or visitation).

The clearly taught biblical norm is that *proclamation brings revelation!* Romans 10:17 says, *"So then faith comes by hearing, and hearing by the word of God."*

In context, this passage is talking about the restoration of the Jewish people. Note the clear progression here: Proclamation *precedes* faith. In our outreaches in the former Soviet Union from 1993 to 2004, I witnessed thousands of Jewish people stand or come forward in altar calls and pray to receive Yeshua as their Messiah. It was in response to the *proclamation* of the Gospel, just as Paul taught. They first heard the Gospel in song, testimony, and clear proclamation of the Gospel, and then they responded as faith rose in their hearts.

This was my personal experience in coming to faith as well. As a child growing up in a typical American Jewish family, I did not know much about Jesus. I had no idea that He was a Jew or that, like me, He had grown up observing Jewish Holy Days and attending Shabbat services at synagogue. I did not know that He said He had been sent to "the lost sheep of Israel." To me, Jesus was a foreign deity—the god of the Christians. I had no more in common with Him than I had with Buddha, Mohammed, Krishna, or any other god.

Of course, I had several friends who were Christians, at least culturally. But we never talked about what our families believed. I was born a Jew, just as they were born Christians, and we never talked about it.

I first heard the Gospel as a teenager while in high school. An assistant wrestling coach I admired was quite open about the fact that he was a committed follower of Jesus. It was clear that something was different about him. He always seemed to be happy and he knew why he was here on this earth and where he was going. He had an unusual peace about him. He led a local chapter for a ministry called Young Life, and one day he invited me to come to the meetings. So I went.

It intrigued me to hear him talk about his faith. I found it compelling that anyone could believe he had such a close, personal relationship with God. Although I wasn't ready yet to make any sort of commit to the Lord at that point, faith was being deposited in my heart through the word of God I was ingesting.

It wasn't until four years later, after the completion of my sophomore year in college that I was again confronted with the Gospel. This time, it was through the dramatic conversion of a friend. Her name was Suzie, and like me, she was searching in all the wrong places: drugs, cults like the Grateful Dead, even the occult. As she got heavier and heavier into drugs, I saw her life ebb away. She lost interest in school, stopped taking care of herself, and became thin and haggard. Eventually, I lost touch with her. When I bumped into her again off-campus a few months later, she was smiling, her eyes sparkled, and she looked neat and clean. "What happened to you?" I asked.

"I've been born again," she said. She proceeded to tell me in great detail how Jesus had taken away her craving for drugs and given her a new life. When she finally paused long enough for me to get a word in edgewise, my response was typical of those who have a subjective worldview: "I'm happy for you," I said. "This is so great for you—but it is not for me."

But whatever had happened to her had not only changed her life but had also turned her into a persistent and rather annoying evangelist. Over the next few weeks she called me every day, asking questions such as, "Do you know why you are here on the earth?" and, "Where would you go if you died right now?" Although I really didn't think I was interested, I found myself answering her calls and talking to her for hours about her new faith and spiritual matters. She eventually invited me to attend a Bible study group she was attending and I, reluctantly, agreed.

From the moment I walked into that basement room in Amherst, New York, I wanted to turn around and run. The study session seemed to go on for hours, although it was probably only around 90 minutes or so. I was miserable. I felt completely out of place and was positive that everyone there was fully aware of my extreme discomfort.

When the meeting finally ended, the leader came over and asked if I would join him in the living room for a few minutes. I really wanted to leave and go home but the living room was upstairs, closer to the exit, so I agreed.

I followed him into the living room and sat on the couch, where we were joined by the older gentleman, who had kissed me on the cheek. He placed a Bible in my lap and began to lead me through the Scriptures, beginning with Romans 3:23: *"For all have sinned and fall short of the glory of God"* (NIV). Interesting.

Then he turned to Romans 6:23: *"For the wages of sin is death, but the gift of God is eternal life in Christ Jesus our Lord."* At that moment I had what I can only refer to as a supernatural experience. While I did not have a vision or hear a heavenly voice, the room became abnormally bright and warm. I began to sweat profusely, and I felt as though that couch had arms that reached out and grabbed me—holding me in place. Suddenly, I was keenly aware of my own separation from a God who loved me and cared about me. He then asked me to pray with him to invite Jesus to come into my life. Although my head said no, my heart was ready. To be honest, I really ended up praying with him to appease him so I could leave rather than because I felt I really wanted to and was ready to make the commitment.

In the days that followed, I had an unquenchable desire to read the Bible. Eventually I found a Bible that contained the New

Testament as well as the Old and began to devour it. From that point on, my life has never been the same. Looking back, I now understand clearly that my pilgrimage really began back in high school attending those Young Life meetings. I was hearing the Word and as Scripture tells us, *"The Word will not return void"* (see Isa. 55:11). Faith was being planted in my heart and that faith was re-activated again four years later when Suzie started to witness to me and invited me to her Bible study. It was at that moment, the second Saturday in May of 1980, that the faith deposited in my heart connected with the confession of my mouth and I was saved (see Rom. 10:9). It was the proclamation of the Gospel, first in high school and then four years later in college that built faith in my heart and ultimately, in God's perfect timing, produced revelation and transformation.

Bringing About the One New Man

By definition, the One New Man is Jew and Gentile joined together, with the wall of hostility between them broken down. It should be obvious that a replacement theology version of a Gentile church in place of Israel is impossible within this definition. Replacing Israel does nothing to break down the wall of hostility, as two millennia of animosity have demonstrated.

By the same definition, the identity of the One New Man must be in Messiah. Dual Covenant theology is incompatible with the One New Man, since it declares that Jews do not need to embrace Yeshua as their Messiah.

I believe all would be better served (not to mention more faithful to the Great Commission) if Christians who love Israel (especially leaders) would embrace the passionate desire of Paul with regard to Israel and forthrightly say, "We are evangelical Christians, compelled to share the Gospel with *all* people. That means we cannot exclude anyone. We will share our faith openly, since this is what God calls us to do. But also know that our love for Jewish people and our support of Israel is unconditional."

I pray that Christian Zionism will continue to grow and flourish. Israel needs our support now more than ever. Hezbollah, Iran, and Syria are not going away. They hate the Jewish state and want to push these "intruders" into the sea.

Anti-Semitism is on the rise worldwide. We need friends certainly, but this friendship cannot be at the expense of withholding the Gospel from those with whom it began. Now is His appointed time "to favor Zion." Now is the time for the Gospel to return to the very ones that were responsible for taking it to the four corners of the earth in the first place.

Be the blessing that God has called and anointed you to be in the lives of the Jewish people you know and will come to know. They are not there by accident. And don't forget...there is no greater blessing you bring to a Jewish person than the gift of eternal life through helping him or her find a relationship with their Messiah. And His name is Yeshua.

The Salvation of Israel and World Redemption

My final thought concerns the connection between the salvation of Israel and the redemption of the world. In Romans 11:11, Paul reiterates for a third time that God is not finished with the Jewish people: *"Did they stumble so as to fall beyond recovery? Not at all!"* (NIV)

The apostle then shares a truth that it is through Israel's rejection of Jesus as Messiah that salvation has now come to the Gentiles. This salvation comes with a debt of responsibility to provoke the Jewish people to jealousy. For this to happen, Christians need to demonstrate, through godly character and lifestyle, that they have the love, joy, peace, and sense of purpose that unbelieving

Jewish people lack and so desperately desire. The problem is that for nearly 2,000 years, the institutional Church has simply provoked the Jewish people, rather than provoking them to jealousy.

He then shares an astonishing revelation in Romans 11:15: *"For if their rejection is the reconciliation of the world, what will their acceptance be but life from the dead?"* (NIV)

Paul is revealing that there is a divine connection between what happens with Israel and what happens in the Church. The destinies of both are interconnected. It was the Jews' rejection of their Messiah that brought salvation to the Gentiles, and it is now their acceptance that will bring *life from the dead.* In other words, the redemption of Israel will bring life from the dead for the Church as well as the entire world, which will then be followed by the return of Messiah to the earth.

So the glorious fulfillment of the One New Man must include the Jews coming to know Yeshua and fulfilling the promise that *"all Israel will be saved."* It's not just about the salvation of a people for the sake of their salvation. More than that, Israel is the key to the redemption of the nations.

Paul tells us that indeed the time will come when *"all Israel will be saved"* (Rom. 11:26) but that day will come only after what Paul calls the *"fullness of the Gentiles com[ing] in"* (Rom. 11:25). I believe he was taking about an end-time fullness coming back to the Body of Christ—a fullness of time, a fullness of revelation, and finally, a fullness of identity.

The fullness of time is evident as the season for the fulfillment of the Gentiles is reaching its culmination. The fullness of revelation is manifested as we recognize and then embrace the fullness of our God-given identity in Yeshua. This fullness is the true picture of the One New Man—Jew and Gentile together, one in the body of Messiah.

CHAPTER 11

The Blessings and Mission of Those Grafted In

Dr. Craig Keener, Asbury Theological Seminary

Romans 11 is a key text for understanding Paul's vision for Jewish and Gentile relations.[1] First of all, it includes the most explicit New Testament[2] text (see Rom. 11:26) about a message earlier prominent in Israel's prophets: that God will turn the Jewish people back to himself (see Amos 9:7-15; Hos. 14:4-7; Deut. 4:30-31). Although there has been some debate about the interpretation of the passage, I believe that Paul's expectation that the Jewish people as a whole will ultimately embrace faith in Jesus is fairly clear here.[3] Second, this passage signals a key shift in Paul's argument in Romans. After assuring Gentile believers in Romans 1 to 10 that they are not spiritually inferior to Jewish believers, Paul now warns Gentile believers to respect the Jewish people and the Jewish heritage into which their new faith has introduced them.

While noting some of these fairly conspicuous points, however, I want to focus in this essay on Paul's teaching about the role of Gentile believers. First, what does it mean for Gentile believers to be grafted into the heritage of Israel? Second, how can Gentile believers serve God's purposes for the Jewish people? In this chapter, Paul suggests that the conversion of Gentiles serves a purpose on behalf of God's plan for his Jewish people, a purpose that has so far usually gone unfulfilled in history.

What Does It Mean for Gentile Believers to Be Grafted In?

Paul does not speak of a new and separate olive tree, either replacing or parallel to the tree whose natural branches are Jewish. Rather, he speaks of believing Gentiles being "grafted in" to the original tree, among the remaining (Messianic Jewish) branches, while unbelieving Jewish branches are broken off.

Gentiles Welcomed in the Tanakh

In the Hebrew Bible, although God maintained his faithfulness to Israel, those Israelites who broke the covenant cut themselves off from it personally; some Gentiles also became part of the Covenant, joining the people of Israel. These Gentiles who embraced the covenant included Rahab the Canaanite, Ruth the Moabitess, and the "strangers in the land," resident aliens who, by settling among the 12 tribes, agreed to abide by their laws. Israelites were to welcome such strangers and treat them as graciously as fellow-Israelites. (See Exodus 22:21; 23:9; Leviticus 19:33-34; 23:22; 24:22; 25:6; Deuteronomy 1:16; 10:18-19; 14:29; 24:17,19-21; 24:14; 26:11, 13; 27:19; Jeremiah 7:6; Ezekiel 22:7; Malachi 3:5.)

Like Israel's genetic descendants, these resident aliens could share in the celebration of Israel's exodus from Egypt (see Exod. 12:19; Num. 9:14); atonement rituals (see Lev. 16:29; Num. 15:26,29; 19:10); the Sabbath (see Exod. 20:10; 23:12); various laws for Israel (see Exod. 20:10; Lev. 17:8-15; 18:26; 20:2; 22:18; 24:16; Num. 15:14-15, 30); and even cities of refuge (see Num. 35:15).

In some respects, such as food (see Deut. 14:21) or land (see Lev. 25:45), the resident alien may have been held to a lower standard, but in most respects they were treated with the same kindness shown to fellow Israelites. These Gentile residents entered the covenant along with ethnic Israel (see Deut. 29:10-15; 31:12), hence dared not follow idols (see Deut. 29:11, 18). In the promised future, they would receive an inheritance among the tribes where they sojourned (see Ezek. 47:22-23). The foreigner who kept God's Sabbaths would not be inferior to those born Jewish; such Gentiles would be better off than Israelites who did not follow God's commands (see Isa. 56:3-5).

The prophets' visions of the future portrayed different destinies for the Gentiles, perhaps depending on the individual peoples' or individuals' response to Israel's God: Gentiles might be subjugated (see Isa. 60:12; Zeph. 2:11); might be destroyed (see Joel 3:19; Zeph. 2:9-15); or, most relevant to our discussion, might repent and somehow join Israel among God's people (see Isa. 19:19-25; Zech. 2:11). Jewish sources from Paul's era also reported a range of perspectives regarding Gentiles in the end-time.[4] But at least some Jewish people recognized that the fulfillment of God's promises would bring an ingathering of Gentiles.

The Debate Over Circumcision

Clearly, Paul has biblical grounds for affirming the welcoming of Gentiles, but his views probably diverged on some key issues from those of his contemporaries. Paul treats Gentiles as spiritual proselytes,[5] grafted into God's people, but without requiring physical circumcision (see Rom. 4:9-13; Gal. 3:29). It is not difficult to see why his approach would have appeared controversial to many of his contemporaries. Before a male resident alien could participate in the Passover, he had to be circumcised (see Exod. 12:48-49). Circumcision was the necessary sign of the covenant (see Gen. 17:10-14); although resident aliens are not mentioned, servants who are members of Israelite households are (see Gen. 17:12-13), and failure to accept circumcision entailed violation of the covenant and being cut off from God's people (see Gen. 17:14).

It is thus not surprising that while many Jews affirmed that some Gentiles could be righteous by avoiding idolatry, sexual immorality, and some other flagrant sins, most affirmed only those who accepted circumcision as true *proselytes* or converts to Judaism. Many Jewish people believed that the former could be saved, but only the latter could become part of the people of God. (In practice, the latter sometimes faced prejudices and were of lower status than those born Jewish, but they nevertheless remained part of God's people.) While circumcision of Gentiles does not feature very prominently in the Hebrew Bible (see Josh. 5:7), it was a crucial issue by Paul's day; many Jewish people had given their lives to resist Antiochus Epiphanes' hostility to circumcision, raising its importance as a notable mark of Jewish identity (see 1 Maccabees 1:15, 60-61; 2:46; 2 Maccabees 6:10; 4 Maccabees 4:25).

Early believers in Jesus who reached out to Gentiles apparently encountered a different reality on the ground. Some Jews would have allowed Gentiles to accept Judaism without circumcision, under some pressing circumstances, though many others disagreed (Josephus, *Antiquities of the Jews* 20.38-44). But in practice in the Diaspora, the line between the more faithful of God-fearing Gentiles attending synagogues and full proselytes may have sometimes appeared thin, and this was probably the case as the Greek-speaking Messianic Jews of Antioch began reaching Gentiles (see Acts 11:19-21).

What quickly became apparent to believers on the cutting edge of evangelism was that God was conferring on Gentiles the promised Spirit without prior circumcision (see Acts 10:44-45; 11:15-18; 15:8-9). God had promised the Spirit to Israel in connection with their future restoration (see Isa. 44:3; 59:20-21; Ezek. 36:24-48; 37:14; 39:28-29; Joel 2:28-29; Zech. 12:10), yet this end-time gift was being poured out on Gentiles! The Hebrew Bible already emphasized internal, spiritual circumcision (see Deut. 10:16; 30:6; Jer. 4:4) and warned that even Israel could be spiritually uncircumcised (see Lev. 26:41; Jer. 9:26). The prophets had also spoken of a New Covenant in which God would establish his laws in the hearts of his people (see Jer. 31:31-34; Ezek. 36:27). For those who believed that the Spirit marked Jesus' followers as the true end-time remnant of Israel, it was clear that God was welcoming Gentile converts as well. The outward sign of the covenant was merely a symbol pointing to the greater end-time experience of the covenant; God accepted Gentiles with the latter whether or not they had the former. For Paul, the experience of end-time reality was so important as to render the outward symbol spiritually superfluous for those who did not already have it—that is, for Gentiles.

Some more conservative believers, however, did not see the present "end-time" situation as changing quite so much, and insisted on more traditional ways. Starting especially from Genesis 17 rather than the Spirit-empowered experience of end-time prophetic fulfillment, their position is very understandable. Some of Paul's rivals followed this approach, perhaps because of pressures back home (see Gal. 6:12; Gal. 5:11). Yet it was problematic on the field, where Gentiles were coming to Israel's God. Because circumcision was painful for adults (babies, of course, had little say in the matter), requiring it could deter converts. It also reflected a very different view of what it took to be members of the Covenant.

Whereas circumcision could deter many Gentiles from conversion, this consideration was not very relevant to the other marker often used alongside it to designate conversion: baptism. Ceremonial washings were common in antiquity, and the sort of Gentile who would convert to Judaism understood that by Jewish standards he or she was impure (tainted by idolatry). Although there has been some debate, it seems fairly certain that Jewish people at least often baptized Gentiles converting to Judaism; Jewish teachers certainly did not borrow the practice from Christians.[6] What seems remarkable is not that Gentiles were immersed when joining Jesus' movement, but that fellow-Jews accepted the same rite of purification (adopted earlier by another Jewish prophet, John).[7]

God-fearers or Proselytes?

Many Jewish people accepted in principle the possibility of righteous Gentiles. They did not believe that God expected Gentiles to keep the laws given to Israel, but they did believe that God had some universal standards communicated to Adam and Noah. These included the avoidance of idolatry and sexual immorality, which were held to characterize most Gentiles. In the Diaspora, many God-fearing Gentiles attended synagogues, and some financially supported synagogues. Probably most of these God-fearers often stopped short of becoming full proselytes, avoiding circumcision and commandments specifically designated for Israel.

When the community of Messianic believers in Jerusalem settled on a handful of requirements for Gentile believers in Acts 15:20 and 29, they were not declaring that these believers were full proselytes. They were simply requesting the minimum requirements for God-fearers observing the rules that tradition claimed that God gave Noah (or the rules for resident aliens in Leviticus). That is, they were agreeing to a compromise solution: Conservative Jewish believers could accept these Gentiles as saved without requiring circumcision, and little was demanded of the Gentiles beyond what they already knew. The solution kept peace, and sometimes that is what believers have to do: find the common ground on which we can agree and then work together despite some disagreements.

But for Paul, Gentiles were not merely the equivalent of righteous Gentiles or synagogue adherents without a stronger heritage in Israel. For Paul, Gentiles who obeyed the Jewish king Jesus were full members of God's people. Paul insisted that believers were spiritual children of Abraham, following his example of faith see Rom. 4; Gal. 3:7-9,14). Paul also speaks of Gentile converts as spiritually circumcised in Romans 2:26, 29 (see Acts 7:51; Col. 2:11), and, though the matter is debated, probably includes them among the spiritually Jewish (see Rom. 2:29).

Further, for Paul, ethnic descent did not guarantee saving participation in the Covenant (see Rom. 9:6-13); loyalty to God's appointed vizier, the Messiah, was necessary for that (see Rom. 3:22-26). Or in the language of Ephesians, Gentiles once alienated from *"citizenship in Israel"* (see Eph. 2:12 NIV) have now been brought near through their loyalty to Christ (i.e., Israel's true king), in and through Christ (see Eph. 2:13), as part of the "One New Humanity" (see Eph. 2:14-16).[8] Many of the key terms applied to all believers together in Ephesians 1:3-14 are descriptions applied to Israel in the Hebrew Bible.

For Paul, then, while circumcision was not wrong in its place (symbolizing Israel's Covenant status), it was irrelevant with respect to salvation, adding nothing to the saving, New Covenant relationship already found in Christ (see 1 Cor. 7:18-19; Gal. 5:6; 6:15; Col. 3:11). Paul also did not require Gentiles to adopt the *kashrut*, the food rules (see Rom. 14; Mark 7:19; perhaps Acts 10:12-15; Col. 2:21), which constituted part of Israel's separation from the nations (see Lev. 11:44-45). These Jewish dietary laws might be healthier than not, or useful for cultural identification, but they were not mandatory.

Paul did not even require them to keep Israel's festivals (see Rom. 14:5-6; Gal. 4:10; Col. 2:16). I confess that this point continues to perplex me; as we have noted, Gentiles in the land were welcome to keep festivals (though Exodus does require circumcision), and in the end time all the nations would celebrate Israel's deliverance at the feast of tabernacles (see Zech. 14:16-19, though this may simply portray Israel's exaltation in a graphic manner).

Moreover, though righteous Gentiles outside the land were not obligated to keep Israel's laws, God seems to have ordained Shabbat to celebrate His finished work of creation before He gave the law to Israel (see Gen. 2:2-3). Perhaps Paul's interest was primarily in meeting the spirit of the law in this case. Many Gentiles, especially slaves, would have no option to avoid work on the seventh day. (Certainly one cannot support a Sunday Sabbath from this passage, or anything in the New Testament, even if some Christians were already meeting on Sundays.)

Paul and the Law

To cynical ears, it may sound like Paul wanted to grant Gentile believers the privileges of proselytes while imposing on them only the requirements of righteous God-fearers. This cynicism, however, underestimates the role of the end-time Spirit in Paul's experience and theology. Paul believed that the spirit of the law remained in force; the transcultural principles that drove its statutes for ancient Israelite society now transformed the heart. For Paul, the law supports his teaching of God transforming us through dependence on Him (being made righteous through faith; Rom. 3:31; Romans 10:6-10, making an analogy with Deuteronomy 30:11-14). The problem is not the law, but treating it as a means of self-justification or boasting (see Rom. 3:27; 7:9-14). Love summarizes the law (see Rom. 13:8-10), and the Spirit writes the law in our hearts (see Rom. 8:2-4). God's heart, that now stood behind the law, is placed in believers' hearts by the Spirit.

As one who teaches hermeneutics, I am often concerned because believers wrongly conform their understanding of the spirit of the law to their own cultural values, an approach that usually causes us to miss Scripture's point. At the same time, I recognize, following the *midrashic* approach of Jesus, as well as of Paul, that the spirit of the law is its primary point. Often these explorations lead to demands morally stricter than in the written Torah (see Matt. 5:21-48; cf. 19:8-9, though I believe there is some hyperbole here).[9] But we must also recognize that God contextualized His principles in particular, concrete forms for His people in particular times in history, including in the Torah. Comparing Israel's laws with second-millennium BCE Mesopotamian legal collections[10] shows that these laws addressed a particular kind of legal milieu; many of the laws also specify their applicability to the land of Israel and specifically address an agrarian society.

The principles behind these laws remain important for us today, but in a new cultural setting we will apply them in new ways. For example, those of us who do not entertain neighbors on flat roofs may not need a parapet around the roof (see Deut. 22:8), but we are still responsible for our neighbor's safety. Rabbinic Judaism chose one approach to updating the laws, lovingly handling individual laws like legal scholars questioning hypothetical cases. The trajectory of Jesus and Paul is different from (though not in every case incompatible with) rabbinic Judaism's, and cannot be followed properly without depending on God's Spirit (see Gal. 5:16, 22-23).

Provoking Israel to Envy

When farmers grafted foreign branches onto trees, they did so partly to strengthen the trees.[11] Grafting the Gentiles into the heritage of Israel is meant to enrich God's plan for his people in history, not to cut down the first tree and plant a new one to supplant it.

While Paul clearly did care about Gentiles for their own sake (see 1 Thess. 3:5-10), he also viewed his Gentile mission as somehow a witness to his own people. Building on a passage from the Torah (which he quotes in Romans 10:19), Paul explains that the conversion of the Gentiles should make his own people jealous (see Rom. 11:11,14). How would it make them jealous? Perhaps because their biblical end-time mission of being a light to the nations was being fulfilled through Paul and others like him; God's promises regarding the nations were being fulfilled through those who followed Jesus as the Messiah![12] Thus, the full measure of Gentiles being saved would precipitate Paul's own people turning to God, hence the completion of salvation history (see Rom. 11:25-27).

It would have made sense to Paul that his people would recognize God at work through his and others' ministry in converting Gentiles. Paul's people knew the biblical promises about vast numbers of Gentiles coming to acknowledge Israel's God (see Isa. 19:19-25; Zech. 2:11); if these new followers of Israel's God came through recognition of Jesus as Israel's king, surely Israel should recognize that God was with this movement bringing so many people to God and righteous behavior.

Many Jewish people expected Israel's end-time repentance and restoration to bring about the ingathering of Gentiles;[13] the first-century Messianic Jewish movement, however, saw themselves as the righteous remnant of Israel who were already repentant, the first fruits of Israel's restoration. (The community that produced many of the Dead Sea Scrolls apparently viewed themselves the same way, although unlike Jesus' followers, they did not claim miracles or massive numbers of Gentile converts to show for their efforts.) Paul also believed that Gentile repentance could provoke Jewish repentance.

Many scholars believe that Paul intended his own offering from his Diaspora churches, brought for the needs of the Jerusalem church (see Rom. 15:26-27), as a partial fulfillment of the promised gifts from the nations (see Isa. 60:9). Some believe that Paul intended this collection as a visible sign of the ingathering of

Gentiles that would constitute a witness to Israel. That plan offers a fairly fitting climax for Paul's argument for the unity of Jewish and Gentile believers in Romans, a theme that ties most of the letter together. Paul begins by arguing that not only Gentiles, but Jewish people, are lost (see Rom. 1-3). He continues that not mere ethnic descent from Abraham but walking in the steps of Abraham's faith is necessary (see Rom. 4:1-5:11); all people (including Abraham's descendants) share a common humanity and can share new life in Christ (see Rom. 5:12-6:23). Further, the law informs us about righteousness but does not transform our character into righteousness (chapter 7), unless written in the heart through the Spirit (see Rom. 7:6; 8:2). The law does not, then, automatically make its possessors into people who are necessarily intrinsically morally superior.

Paul traces salvation history in chapters 9-11, showing in chapter 9 that God is not bound to choose for salvation based on one's ethnic heritage, and in chapter 11 that His plan for his Jewish people remains intact. He quickly turns to praxis: All believers must serve one another (see Rom. 12), and must respect the heart of the law, namely love (see Rom. 13:8-10). Believers must stop looking down on one another's food customs and holy days (see Rom. 14). They can recognize as examples of Jewish-Gentile unity both Yeshua (see Rom. 15:7-12) and Paul himself (see Rom. 15:15-25), especially in view of the collection (see Rom. 15:25-27). His closing exhortation includes avoiding division (see Rom. 16:17).

Provoking Contempt Instead of Envy: Christendom and Anti-Semitism

Paul expected the ingathering of Gentiles to make his people jealous, to recognize that God was at work in Jesus' movement so they would embrace that movement themselves. Yet through most of history, most Jewish people have affirmed trust in Jesus as Messiah as a belief suited only for Gentiles, not for their own people. Although many more Jewish people affirm Jesus as Messiah today than through the vast majority of history, they still constitute a small proportion of the Jewish People, and the response of his people clearly has never yet been what Paul hoped. What went wrong? Why did the proliferation of faith in Israel's one true God among the Gentiles not serve as a witness to Israel? I believe that it is largely because Gentile Christians ignored Paul's other teachings in the same context.

Our histories diverged as Jesus' movement spread among Gentiles, but given what Gentile Christians shared with Jewish People as a whole (both a shared heritage and an ethical monotheism that contrasted starkly with the rest of the Gentile world), the divergence proved unexpectedly harsh and tragic in ways Paul could not have foreseen.

Paul's Warning

Paul's vision of Gentile believers provoking Israel's turn to the Messiah did not fail in principle; it was simply never tried the way Paul articulated it. Paul's appeal to Israel involved repentant Gentiles turning to the God and Messiah of Israel; what arose instead was a Gentile church that conveniently forgot from whom they learned about God and the Messiah. Note what Paul wrote to Gentiles grafted in as wild branches to the olive tree: Do not be arrogant against the natural branches; God could graft back in the fallen natural branches more easily than he grafted you in to begin with. Moreover, if you are arrogant, God can cut you off as he cut off the natural branches (see Rom. 11:17-24). What Paul warned Gentiles against doing is precisely what subsequent generations proceeded to do, ignoring his warning.

Anti-Judaism abounded in the Roman world, especially among Greeks; writers like Apion falsely accused Judaism of terrible atrocities.[14] Roughly a decade after Paul wrote, many Gentile communities in the Roman province of Syria slaughtered their

Jewish populations, and a few decades later Alexandria slaughtered and drove out its tens of thousands of Jewish residents.

Those converted to Christianity from anti-Jewish backgrounds typically displayed little desire to affirm their new Jewish heritage, and accommodating their perspectives brought anti-Judaism into the Church. Though few interpreters went as far as Marcion (who rejected the Old Testament and the God of Israel outright), many Gentile Christians accepted Christ (Israel's promised King) while rejecting His people. These Gentiles often argued that their movement had supplanted the Jewish people in God's plan, that the Jewish people had forfeited hope of restoration, or the like. Indeed, instead of Jewish believers being grafted back into their own tree, later Gentile Christians often expected them to be grafted into Gentile Christianity, adopting Gentile customs as a sign of faith in their own Jewish Messiah. They could be forced to formally renounce everything Jewish and their connections with it. The polarization between Gentile Christians and non-Messianic Judaism pulled prospective believers in contradictory directions; establishing a distinctively Messianic Jewish identity in such settings was difficult.

In later centuries, sometimes Gentiles persecuted or even killed Jewish people in the name of Christianity.[15] The subsequent history of Christendom in the West is stained with the blood of vast numbers of Jewish people drowned in "baptisms," crucified, tortured by the Inquisition, and so forth. While God's grace is evident in much of Christian history, the Christian doctrine to which it often testifies most eloquently is human depravity.

Replacements, or Messianic Gentiles?

"Grafted in" spiritual proselytes are honored by being welcomed into God's people; proselytes are not, however, usurpers. Much of Christendom, through most of Christian history, viewed the Church as a replacement for Israel. They typically viewed membership in the Church as salvific in the same way that the Jewish community had viewed membership in Israel as salvific—the very sort of arrogance that Paul denounced. For Paul, salvation was through faithful dependence on Christ, not through ethnicity or membership in a particular social group apart from such faith.

The problem was already incipiently present in Paul's day. Ancient sources reveal that Roman Gentiles looked down on Jewish people especially for circumcision, Sabbaths, and food customs.[16] Paul warns Jewish and Gentile believers to allow for differences in such customs and to respect one another's practices (see Rom. 14:3-13). Instead of looking down on one another, we should welcome one another (see Rom. 15:7) and glorify God together in unity (see Rom. 15:6).

All Gentile believers should recognize and affirm our common heritage with the Jewish people. I am not suggesting that all Gentile believers should join Messianic congregations. There are two reasons why I would not suggest this. First, Paul clearly articulates a principle of cultural sensitivity: Each culture must be welcome to embrace the Messiah Yeshua in ways that are culturally relevant to their own community. This is part of their witness to their own people, to draw more members of all peoples to the one true God. But second, even if all Jewish people believed in Yeshua and attended Messianic congregations, Gentile believers far outnumber them, and Gentile believers' numbers would simply overwhelm them and their culture. For pragmatic reasons, then, we should not expect all Gentile believers to join Messianic congregations, but only those who feel especially led to identify with the Messianic movement's identity and witness to the Jewish people.

At the same time, all Gentile believers should recognize their heritage and the biblical obligation to respect the Jewish people. It should go without saying that love for neighbor obligates us to stand with any of our neighbors who faces injustice; to affirm that

Christians should work against anti-Semitism should therefore be obvious even to those who do not agree with our interpretation of Romans 11. Love for neighbor is in the synagogue's canon as well; when I was an associate minister in an African-American congregation that had received threats of violence for speaking out against racism, the rabbi of a local synagogue offered to surround our church with his members to help defend us. That was a costly expression of love for neighbor.

Paul's plan never succeeded because it was never really implemented. What might happen today if Gentile Christians were to show the Jewish people that we have come to faith in Israel's God? What might happen if we expressed appreciation to the Jewish people for sharing their God with the rest of humanity, most of whom once worshiped or feared many lesser gods? If we affirmed that we embraced rather than usurped their heritage? Whatever the response might be today, after so many centuries of anti-Semitism, we owe it both to the Jewish people and to our Lord Jesus to offer this recognition.

Most Jewish people will not care whether Gentiles keep Shabbat (Jewish tradition even developed a useful place for helpful Gentiles who do *not* keep the Sabbath). But it would be a major step forward if both the Jewish and Christian communities understood Jesus' followers as loyal and obedient to Israel's God and to the Jewish messianic claimant Jesus[17] as King of humanity. Because of Messianic Jews reaching Gentiles, Israel's one God now has hundreds of millions of followers around the world.

Like everything else in U.S. culture, our Christianity is consumer- and market-driven, which leaves short memories for matters like heritage; it leaves us with a historically truncated faith. The positive side of that mostly negative situation is that little loyalty remains to any anti-Jewish heritage of Christendom, so that we are free to appeal to a better heritage flowing from the beginning of our Lord's movement.

The Value of a Continuing Messianic Jewish Witness

Many Jewish people are becoming followers of Jesus today. Like anyone else, they are free to choose the place and style of worship that they find most suitable. At the same time, children raised in Gentile churches usually assimilate, losing much of their distinctive Jewish identity and heritage over time. Messianic Judaism provides a context where Jewish followers of Yeshua can affirm both their faith in Yeshua and the rest of their Jewish heritage. They are, in Paul's words, grafted back into their own natural tree, and this setting provides a means of affirming that identity.

Because it has been controversial, Messianic Judaism has sometimes proved an obstacle in dialogue between the larger Jewish and Christian communities, but we must persevere in making it a bridge. From the Christian side, a key issue in theological discussion with the Jewish community remains the identity of the Messiah; from the standpoint of a significant proportion of the Jewish community, however, one can be Jewish without believing that there *is* a Messiah or there *is* a resurrection from the dead (contra Maimonides or the Mishnah). Among key concerns for most of the Jewish community are identity and boundaries: One can believe a variety of things, but once one believes that Jesus is the Messiah, this makes one a "Christian," hence one belongs to a Gentile religion that is defined in opposition to Judaism and assimilates into Gentile culture.

This understanding of Jesus' movement certainly does not rest on our foundational records of his earliest followers. Jesus' first followers were a Messianic Jewish movement who began reaching massive numbers of Gentiles. Given the explosive growth of the movement, Messianic Jews probably quickly outnumbered Pharisees, of whom Josephus says there were only 6,000 (*Antiquities of the Jews* 17.42; see Acts 21:20).[18] Many scholars today even argue that Paul and his colleagues represent an earlier form of Judaism than what we find in the Talmud (which was certainly written much later than Paul's day). Far from Jews and Christians being mutually exclusive categories in the beginning, most early followers of Jesus were Jewish, and they neither saw nor should have seen any contradiction. Gentile Christians cannot repudiate Messianic Judaism without repudiating the apostolic foundations of their own faith.

Judaism and Gentile Christianity subsequently went their separate ways, however, as we have noted. Thus one friend who is an Orthodox rabbi insisted that we must respect the boundaries that history has drawn between the two religions. He did not mean that Jews and Christians should not get along, but he rejected the possibility of a person being both Jewish and a believer in Jesus. My response was that if we pronounce the groups separate based on their history after their origins, we should now pronounce them overlapping based on their current history. (We had to agree to disagree for the time being.)

In one location where I lived some years ago, I often attended a Conservative synagogue led by a very knowledgeable Reconstructionist rabbi, who always welcomed me graciously. (His congregation's Torah services were also greatly improving my Hebrew.) One evening he was complaining about the Orthodox in Israel rejecting the Jewish identity of those who had Jewish fathers but not Jewish mothers, even though the Jewishness of these children was accepted by less conservative Jewish groups. He insisted that it was unfair to reject the Jewish identity of those who identified themselves as Jewish. Afterward I asked whether this argument would be consistent with rejecting the Jewishness of Messianic believers. He replied that it would be, because they do not observe Jewish customs like the *kashrut* and holy days. Sidestepping the separate question as to whether he would exclude nonobservant Jews, I pointed out that I knew Messianic Jews who did keep these customs. He acquiesced that perhaps then they were still Jewish. I do not know whether I persuaded him permanently, but some others with whom I have spoken have made similar observations. Some Jewish scholars have suggested that non-Orthodox Jews who welcome as fellow Jews those less *halakhically* observant and theistic than Messianic Jews are inconsistent to refuse Messianic Jews.[19]

If Jewish people choose to believe in Yeshua, what better guard can be provided against assimilation and abandonment of Jewish identity than Messianic Judaism? The question of Jesus' identity should be able to be discussed without the baggage of two millennia of Gentile Christendom that often departed starkly from Jesus' own message. I believe that Messianic Judaism provides that bridge, a witness for Yeshua to the Jewish people, and for the Jewish people to Gentile Christians.

Conclusion

Grafted into the heritage of Israel, Gentile believers have experienced innumerable blessings resting on earlier salvation history and God's promises. At the same time, Gentile believers have a role and a mission to show the Jewish people loyalty to the God and heritage of Israel—not to displace the Jewish people but to attract them. It is through the message of Jesus, announced by his first followers as the true Davidic king, that Gentile believers have come to worship the one God of Israel and embrace Israel's Scriptures.

Paul expected that the turning of vast numbers of Gentiles to faith in Israel's God would persuade many of his people that Jesus was, after all, the Messiah his witnesses claimed him to be. Through most of history, however, Gentile Christians have neglected Paul's warning to respect their Jewish heritage and the Jewish "branches." By treating themselves as Israel's successors, they have both laid themselves open to ancient Israel's temptations and despised their Lord's own people. Christian anti-Semitism injured and alienated the Jewish people even as it corrupted the Church by explicit disobedience to both the letter and spirit of Jesus' message. A new era is dawning, with new opportunities for dialogue. May we learn from Scripture and from the past.

Endnotes

1. I have treated this chapter, and Romans as a whole, in fuller detail (though with a different focus) in Craig S. Keener, *Romans* (Eugene, OR: Cascade/Wipf & Stock, 2009).

2. I use this term for lack of a better one; everyone should understand that mention of a new covenant in some early Christian books no more makes them a covenant themselves than mention of it in Jeremiah makes the Hebrew Bible into a new or renewed covenant itself.

3. See e.g., discussion in A. Andrew Das, *Paul and the Jews* (Peabody: Hendrickson, 2003), 96-106; Terence L. Donaldson, *Paul and the Gentiles: Remapping the Apostle's Convictional World* (Minneapolis: Fortress, 1997), 231-234; Keener, *Romans*, 136-38.

4. See Donaldson, *Paul and the Gentiles*, 52-74.

5. See especially Donaldson, *Paul and the Gentiles*, 230-47.

6. See discussion in Craig Keener, *The Gospel of John: A Commentary* (2 vols.; Peabody: Hendrickson, 2003), 445-447 and sources cited there (e.g., *t. A.Z.* 3:11; Epictetus *Disc.* 2.9.20; I. Abrahams, *Studies in Pharisaism and the Gospels*, 1st series [New York: KTAV, 1967], 37, 42; C. G. Montefiore, *The Synoptic Gospels* [2 vols.; New York: KTAV, 1968], 1:8; Lawrence H.

Schiffman, "At the Crossroads: Tannaitic Perspec-
tives on the Jewish Christian Schism," 2:115-56 in
Jewish and Christian Self-Definition [3 vols.; ed. E. P.
Sanders; Philadelphia: Fortress, 1980-1982], 128).

7. John's practice of immersing his people appears
even outside the New Testament, in Jos. *Ant.* 18.117
(although Josephus adapts it in such a way as to appeal
to his Hellenistic audience).

8. This "One New Man" probably plays further on
Paul's theology of the new Adam: While Jewish people are descended from Abraham (see Rom. 4), all are
descended from Adam (see Rom 5:12-21). Believers
should live dead to the old humanity in Adam, putting on the new humanity, recreated in God's image in
Christ (see Eph 4:21-24; Rom 5:12-21; 6:3-6).

9. See discussion in Craig S. Keener, *The Gospel of Matthew: A Socio-Rhetorical Commentary* (Grand Rapids: Eerdmans, 2009), 175-205, 465-469.

10. As scholars commonly do; see e.g., Nahum M. Sarna,
Exploring Exodus: The Heritage of Biblical Israel (New
York: Schocken, 1986).

11. Commentators cite Columella *Arb.* 5.9.16 and other
sources; see further discussion in A. G. Baxter and
J. A. Ziesler, "Paul and Arboriculture: Romans 11:17-24,"
JSNT 24 (1985): 25-32.

12. Cf. here Mark D. Nanos, *The Mystery of Romans: The
Jewish Context of Paul's Letter* (Minneapolis: Fortress, 1996), 249-50.

13. See Dale C. Allison, "Romans 11:11-15: A Sugges-
tion," *PRSt* 12 (1985); E. P. Sanders, *Jesus and Judaism*

(Philadelphia: Fortress, 1985), 93. Jewish people did not all agree as to whether the ingathering involved proselytes or righteous Gentiles (Terence Donaldson, "Proselytes or 'Righteous Gentiles'? The Status of Gentiles in Eschatological Pilgrimage Patterns of Thought," *JSP* 7 [1990]: 3-27).

14. For varying approaches to Gentile anti-Judaism in antiquity (alongside some friendlier attitudes), see e.g., J. N. Sevenster, *The Roots of Pagan Anti-Semitism in the Ancient World* (NovTSup 41; Leiden: Brill, 1975); Jerry L. Daniel, "Anti-Semitism in the Hellenistic-Roman Period," *JBL* 98 (1, March 1979): 45-65; John G. Gager, *The Origins of Anti-Semitism: Attitudes Toward Judaism in Pagan and Christian Antiquity* (New York: Oxford University Press, 1983); for examples, see e.g., Cicero *Flacc.* 28.69; Tacitus *Hist.* 5.1-5; Flaccus in Philo *Flacc.* 85.

15. For a history of Christendom's complicity in anti-Semitism, see, e.g., Edward H. Flannery, *The Anguish of the Jews: Twenty-three Centuries of Anti-Semitism* (New York: Macmillan, 1965); James Parkes, *The Conflict of the Church and the Synagogue: A Study in the Origins of Antisemitism* (New York: Atheneum, 1979). For a Messianic Jewish work addressing especially the church, see Michael L. Brown, *Our Hands Are Stained with Blood: The Tragic Story of the "Church" and the Jewish People* (Shippensburg, PA: Destiny Image, 1992).

16. See especially Juvenal *Sat.* 14.96-106.

17. Against a number of scholarly arguments to the contrary, I would agree with those who affirm that Jesus claimed to be Messiah (see Craig S. Keener,

The Historical Jesus of the Gospels (Grand Rapids: Eerdmans, 2009), 256-267).

18. In a population of as much as 500,000, by the older estimate in Marcel Simon, *Jewish Sects at the Time of Jesus* (Philadelphia: Fortress, 1967), 15. Josephus, never known to underestimate numbers, estimates only about 4,000 Essenes (Ant. 18.20).

19. See Dan Cohn-Sherbok, *Messianic Judaism* (New York, London: Cassell, 2000), 169-213 (esp. 174, 203-213); more concisely, idem, "Introduction," ix-xx in *Voices of Messianic Judaism: Confronting Critical Issues Facing a Maturing Movement* (ed. Dan Cohn-Sherbok; Baltimore: Lederer, 2001), xiii-xiv (esp. regarding "pluralists"); slightly earlier, Carol Harris-Shapiro laid out the evidence thoroughly and eloquently in *Messianic Judaism: A Rabbi's Journey through Religious Change in America* (Boston: Beacon, 1999), 166-189. The carefully thought out works of both Harris-Shapiro and Cohn-Sherbok appear to me invaluable for this discussion.

CHAPTER 12

Finding the
One Heartbeat

Coach Bill McCartney, Promise Keepers, Founder

"Why did you leave Promise Keepers?"

Many have asked that question. And because the only way I know to answer people is honestly and directly, I will tell you.

I left Promise Keepers in 2003 because the vision I originally embraced wasn't happening.

Promise Keepers was birthed from a conversation with Dr. Dave Wardell. We were in a car together, driving to a Fellowship of Christian Athletes banquet in Pueblo, Colorado. For the sake of conversation on the two-hour drive, I asked Dr. Wardell, "If you could do anything with your life, money notwithstanding, what would you do?"

He instantly responded, "Disciple men. I would meet with them on street corners, take them into coffee shops, and lead them into a deeper walk with Jesus Christ. How about you?"

I responded that I believed God could fill stadiums with men if we went and got them. From that conversation, Promise Keepers became a reality. And soon stadiums were filled with tens of thousands of men being challenged and changed by the power of God.

Promise Keepers was a unique move of God's Spirit, poured out at such a magnitude that the entire nation took notice. Up to 50,000 men at a time gathered in stadiums across the country, a unified voice used as an instrument of God for catalytic change in America. At the peak of national attention, an estimated one million men converged on the National Mall in Washington, D.C. We did not come to protest or agitate, but to repent before the nation for not fulfilling our biblical mandate as men of God, and to commit ourselves to being the Church that God commanded us to be.

Promise Keepers was a unique call to demonstrate unity in the body of Christ, to become an example of the One New Man of Ephesians 2:15, millions of men acting with one heartbeat.

In many ways, Promise Keepers was immensely successful. I used to sit in the front row at events and weep as I heard great preachers proclaim the Word of God. But something vital was missing.

What was in my heart was not simply thousands of filled seats. The vision I saw involved unity at the deepest level. If you believe in Jesus and you are born of the Spirit, and I also believe in Jesus and that I'm born of the Spirit, then we will spend eternity together. This being true, we should have each other's backs here on Earth. We should be covering each other. There should be a trust level beyond the world's comprehension.

That one heartbeat wasn't happening. Stadiums were filled. The lives of men were changed dramatically. But after the event, the unity that should have characterized our lives just wasn't happening. I left Promise Keepers because I did not see that bonding of the brotherhood. As a football coach, I knew the meaning of one heartbeat on the team, and I didn't see it.

The Cross of Unity

Dr. Henry Blackaby, perhaps best known for the series *Experiencing God*, was invited to speak to our staff. At that time we had over 350 full-time people handling Promise Keepers operations. Dr. Blackaby was scheduled to spend two days with us.

I did not know Dr. Blackaby prior to that meeting. But he spoke a message directly to me that I have never let go of. As he stood before the staff, he said, "After I had prepared my messages for today and tomorrow, I asked the Lord, do you have anything specific that you want me to say to Promise Keepers? And then I did what I always do. I read Matthew, Mark, Luke, and John—the four evangelists. I read only the red print, the words of Jesus, and I waited for Jesus' words to come off the Bible into my heart."

He then described how a passage that he had read thousands of times leaped from the page. It was in the passage describing the moment on the way to Calvary when Simon the Cyrene was given the cross to carry for Jesus for a season.

Dr. Blackaby said, "Almighty God spoke to me and told me that he has given the cross of unity to Bill McCartney."

Unity was the thing missing. We had large crowds at our events, and everyone loved being together, but I did not see the kind of diversity that should have been there. I traveled with Dr. Raleigh Washington to 55 major cities to meet with pastors of color, kneeling at their feet to hear their hearts. They said to me, "Coach, your heart seems okay, but we don't trust those white guys. They can't be reading from the same Bible. They build big churches and have extravaganzas, but they don't seem to notice that we can't even feed our flocks. They don't seem to notice." My heart broke when I heard these words. I realized we were neglecting our brothers.

After Dr. Blackaby's message, I went to the waiting room. I knew that Isaiah 40:31 says, *"Those who wait on the LORD shall renew their strength; They shall mount up with wings like eagles, they shall run and not be weary, they shall walk and not faint."*

Waiting means being ready, standing in a position from which you can move in any direction. Mounting with wings like eagles means flying at a panoramic level where you can see everything.

I also knew that Israel, as they journeyed through the desert on the way to the Promised Land, followed the pillar of cloud that demonstrated God's presence. They did not move without it:

> *Whether it was two days or a month or a year that the cloud lingered over the tabernacle, staying above it, the sons of Israel remained camped and did not set out; but when it was lifted, they did set out* (Numbers 9:22 NASB).

So I went to the waiting room with the cross of unity and cried out to God. "Lord, where's the one heartbeat. How are we going to heal the divide?"

Waiting for the Glory

A few years ago, Dr. Washington and I met in New York City with 16 theologians. They represented the entire spectrum of the Church, from the most conservative branch to the most prophetic, including Jewish believers. They were there to spend a day and a half seeking the meaning of a single verse—John 17:21. In the discussion of that verse, I found what God had me in the waiting room for.

It is the high priestly prayer of Jesus. It is the culminating prayer of His ministry, and a prophetic prayer for the future of

His Church. In that chapter, Jesus prayed for His disciples and for those who would be touched by their ministry in centuries to come. He expressed what was vitally important to Him in His last hours before the cross. In particular, there are three key verses in which Jesus unveils His eternal purpose.

> *I do not pray for these alone, but also for those who will believe in Me through their word; that they all may be one, as You, Father, are in Me, and I in You; that they also may be one in Us, that the world may believe that You sent Me. And the glory which You gave Me I have given them, that they may be one just as We are one* (John 17:20-22).

The biblical path to worldwide revival is right there: "that they may also be one in Us, that the world may believe." Unity is the key to changing the world—all believers in one accord. This prayer of Jesus for His followers includes everyone, Jew and Gentile. "These" were the Jewish followers who were with Him at that moment. "Those" were the Gentiles who would follow, all who would hear His voice.

In this verse Jesus says that He has given them the glory He had received from the Father. In Hebrew, the word glory is *kavod*. It means weightiness or heaviness. It describes a spiritual and tangible presence of God.

In other words, Jesus said that when we become one, God will draw near. That's what happened at Pentecost. A small group of believers gathered together in one accord, with one heart, and the *kavod*, the tangible presence of God, fell on them.

Suddenly, these same disciples who were scattered in fear in the Garden, had been transformed into fearless and courageous men. Their world was changed because the tangible presence of God overpowered them. The presence of God came when they became one. These men experienced God and became Promise Keepers.

Not long after Pentecost, the glory of God fell again in another place. This incident is not talked about as often, but it may be even more significant. The *kavod* fell on a family of Gentiles (see Acts 10:44-48).

That was something unthinkable for Jewish believers at the time. The first church was entirely Jewish. Yeshua came to the lost sheep of Israel. He was Jewish. Jews were taught from childhood that they should not associate with Gentiles.

To overcome this prejudice, God showed the apostle Peter a vision. In the vision, Peter was told to kill and eat animals considered unclean in Jewish law. Peter naturally said no. He was a good Jewish boy. He had never eaten anything unclean in his life.

The voice of God said, "Do not call anything impure that God has made clean." Immediately after that, messengers arrived with an invitation to visit the house of a Gentile named Cornelius.

Peter shared the good news of the Gospel with Cornelius and his family, and the Holy Spirit fell on them the same way He had fallen on Jewish believers at Pentecost. Peter saw the tangible presence of God come when he met in one accord with those lost Gentile sheep Jesus prayed for in John.

By Honor Division Is Healed

Cornelius had long shown favor to Jews. In the tenth chapter of Acts, we find that he was generous to those in need and that he prayed consistently. He honored God's chosen people. In return, God showed him favor through the Jewish believer Peter. When the glory of God fell on him, God confirmed that He wanted Jew and Gentile to walk together.

It seems reasonable to conclude that Cornelius aligned himself with Jewish believers as he lived his faith in the Jewish Messiah. At least for a moment in history, on a small scale, the ideal of the One New Man was a reality.

The word spoken to me by Dr. Blackaby awakened in me a longing for restoration of that ideal. When I returned to Promise Keepers in 2008, I arrived with a burning passion to see one heartbeat in the body of Christ, and that desire has brought a change in focus.

Recently, as many as 10,000 men and women gathered for a Promise Keepers (PK) outdoor conference in Boulder, Colorado. The program platform for this event, "A Time to Honor," focused on three planks taken from the three people groups described in Galatians 3:28. This passage explains that we are neither male nor female, slave nor free, Jew nor Gentile, but all one in Christ Jesus. Scripture instructs us to be in unity.

However, much like Peter before the vision and the command not to call unclean what God has declared otherwise, it has been unthinkable for many to look at every other human being as worthy of honor. In particular, women, the poor, and Jewish believers are being dishonored and devalued both in and out of the Body of Christ. We are far from experiencing genuine biblical unity.

By choosing to honor life and by blessing those people who have not been honored, Promise Keepers determined to become an instrument for healing the divide in the body. By choosing to honor and to bless, we hoped to see the *kavod* of God fall on believers with such power that people would fall on their faces the way they did when the glory filled Solomon's temple.

As we search Scripture for what to do about disunity, we can begin with First Corinthians 12. This chapter teaches that it is by honor that division is healed. Division occurs when one part of the body mistakenly determines that another part is not needed. Healing occurs when honor is extended and all parts of the body are incorporated into the life of the whole.

But now there are many members, but one body. And the eye cannot say to the hand, "I have no need of you"; or again the head to the feet, "I have no need of you." On the contrary, it is much truer that the members of the body which seem to be weaker are necessary; and those members of the body which we deem less honorable, on these we bestow more abundant honor, and our less presentable members become much more presentable, whereas our more presentable members have no need of it. But God has so composed the body, giving more abundant honor to that member which lacked, so that there may be no division in the body, but that the members may have the same care for one another (1 Corinthians 12:20-25 NASB).

Giving honor is not a formula that we recite and get blessing in return. Rather, giving honor to those who have been dishonored comes from an understanding of who God is and who He has called us to be. By submitting to that, we see the glory fall, just as Peter and Cornelius did.

Neither is giving honor simply a matter of making a public acknowledgment of someone's value. That is a place to start, but true honor comes when we then choose to stand side by side, assisting each other in ministry. Unity is seen in service. When the glory falls, the heartbeat of God becomes the one heartbeat of His people. And His heartbeat is for redemption and restoration, for service.

We began to see God's heartbeat in Boulder. By following the admonition in this passage to honor those who are being dishonored, Promise Keepers sought to pursue a model for biblical unity through the three planks of "A Time to Honor." Each plank addressed one of the groups identified in Galatians—women, the poor, and Jews.

Honoring Women

To implement the first plank, we invited women to attend a Promise Keepers event for the first time. As a catalytic ministry to men, the ladies who attended helped us make history. This portion of the conference was powerful. Men were reminded that the Bible calls us to serve women—to undergird them—to build them up so they can be all God intends.

Jane Hansen Hoyt, president of the influential women's ministry Aglow International, became the first woman to speak at a Promise Keepers gathering. She and other speakers reminded us that God created men and women to stand together. "Have you ever wondered why there is such hatred and violence against women?" Jane asked. "One out of every three women experience verbal or sexual abuse from those who profess to love them."

How can we expect the glory of God to fall on us when we allow half of the Church to exist in such a place of restriction and danger? How can we expect to see the world evangelized when we blindly ignore the fact that a number of cultures around the world use religion and tradition as an excuse for dishonoring women? At Boulder, we acknowledged that God has charged us with the responsibility for women reaching the potential for which God created them. We are commanded to stand side by side with them in service.

Jesus set the example when He spoke with the Samaritan women at the Jacob's well. He radically ignored the cultural standards that marginalized women and actually spoke to her. At Boulder, we challenged the current standards in which the Church has been comfortable. Moms, single moms, widows, grandmothers, wives, and single women were honored.

Honoring the Poor

Next, plank two unpacked the biblical mandate for each of us to reach out to the "least of these." Paul declares that in Christ, there is neither slave nor free. A slave is someone who does not have a choice in who his master is going to be. He becomes enslaved to an individual or a process that dictates every part of his life.

In America, we do not have slavery in the same way it existed when Paul wrote to the Galatians, but we see all around us people whose freedom has been taken from them. Circumstances and financial considerations have eliminated the freedom of choice from their lives.

Those whom God has blessed and even prospered must support the poor, oppressed, and needy. James 1:27 says, *"Pure and undefiled religion in the sight of our God and Father is this: to visit orphans and widows in their distress, and to keep oneself unstained by the world"* (NASB). By honoring the poor around us, we help to restore to them the freedom of choice and the ability for them to stand with us in service.

This plank was presented expertly, and specific, proven models were shared to show how men and women can help their churches become involved in transforming their cities by honoring and serving those in need.

Honoring Jews

The third and final plank called for an end to 1900 years of oppression. The Jews in the early church gave the Gospel to us, the Gentiles. These fathers of the faith literally laid down their lives—for both Jew and Gentile. Yet, so many years ago, dishonor erupted. Amazingly, the resulting breach festers and has never been healed.

Remembering that six million Jews perished in the Holocaust—and reminding everyone that each Jew was forced to wear a yellow star sewn on their clothing to identify them for a horrifying destruction—we stood as "those Gentiles" from our Lord's prayer in John 17, and we were challenged to repent for this tragic event and to indicate that we would "never again" stand by if any Jew was persecuted for his faith.

A mythical legend provided some of the inspiration for this part of the Boulder event. The popular version of the story says that King Christian X of Denmark, upon hearing of the German orders for Jews to wear yellow stars, began wearing one on his own arm, prompting other non-Jews to do the same. According to the legend, Germans found it difficult to identify Jews in Denmark and the order became ineffective.

Behind this legend lies an inspiring and challenging reality. The Germans did give orders for Jews to wear yellow stars. The Danes, with great courage and heroism, defied Hitler by sheltering as many Jews as possible from the destruction that swept Europe. King Christian X did resist the German occupation at great risk for both himself and his nation, and became known as a protector of the Jews. As a result, the order to wear yellow stars was never implemented in Denmark. Gentiles there set a precedent of great courage and integrity.

The yellow star became a symbol of the efforts to destroy the Jewish people. Our goal at the event in Boulder was to turn it into a symbol of solidarity between Jew and Gentile. We asked a simple question. Were we willing to give our lives for our Jewish brethren? Non-Jewish believers were invited to come forward, accept a yellow star from Messianic Jewish believers, and wear it as a declaration of one heartbeat.

Something glorious happened in the heavenlies. The honoring of Jews was confirmed by an overwhelming presence of the Holy

Spirit. Men and women poured out of the stadium seats and made their way to the front to receive a yellow star. It was a momentous and life-changing moment as both Jew and Gentile believers united in a time of heartfelt ministry to one another. I could see one heartbeat.

To fully grasp the significance of that moment, it is helpful to examine how the Old Testament ends:

> *Behold, I am going to send you Elijah the prophet before the coming of the great and terrible day of the LORD." He will restore the hearts of the fathers to their children and the hearts of the children to their fathers, so that I will not come and smite the land with a curse* (Malachi 4:5-6 NASB).

The turning of the hearts of children and fathers to each other is necessary to experience the blessings of God. I believe that there is a spiritual application of this verse that we have overlooked. In a very real sense, the Jewish believers of the early church are the spiritual fathers of all followers of Yeshua.

Consider that the Bible was inspired by God through Jewish authors. Consider the passages in which Paul identifies himself as a father to the Gentile believers to whom he was sent as an apostle: *"For in Christ Jesus I became your father through the Gospel"* (1 Cor. 4:15b NASB).

God wants to turn the hearts of the spiritual children, Gentile believers, to the hearts of their spiritual fathers, Jewish believers.

This turning of the spiritual fathers' hearts toward their spiritual children happened at the event in Boulder. Emphatically, God used the giving and receiving of the yellow stars to honor Jews, tenderize hearts, and begin a spiritual healing.

Surely, the path has been cleared for true unity to emerge as a result of the spiritual healing modeled during the presentation of plank three in Boulder. I believe this powerful unity, achieved through honor, will indeed provoke nonbelieving Jews to jealousy. If so, could a revival in Israel be far behind?

One Heartbeat and the Future of the Church

The question at Boulder was, "Would you die to protect your Jewish brother?" People came forward and said, "Yes, I would die." Now we need to ask, how will we live between now and the time we might have to die? Saying we will die someday, if the circumstances require it, and then walking off to ignore our Jewish brothers until that time is not one heartbeat. How then, shall we live?

Finding the one heartbeat means that we live together as One New Man to honor these three planks:

1. We choose to be intentional in honoring women in our society. We encourage those in other societies to do the same.

2. We choose to be intentional about finding people lacking the necessities of life and helping them and blessing them. We teach others to do the same.

3. We choose to be intentional about finding Jewish people who don't know the Lord and we extend honor and love to them. We find those who do know the Lord and we partner with them in serving.

Jesus changed the world in which He lived. He honored women. He spoke to women because they mattered to Him. He made a radical departure from the culture of His time.

Jesus honored the poor. Through the ages, the poor have suffered similar persecution as women. This was a radical departure from the society of the time.

Jesus honored Gentiles. The centurion whose servant Jesus healed was Roman. In at least two cases—one from Samaria and one from Syrophoenicia—the women to whom Jesus spoke were not Jewish. This was a radical departure from Jewish culture.

This world of honoring women, the poor, and Jews is the world that Jesus gave us. He threw away humanity's previous textbook and adjusted our world to the Holy Scriptures. This world did not exist before Jesus. He gave us the three planks of Galatians as a place to stand in our service to this world.

Honor heals, and that healing will initiate a united Church. God's vision for the body of believers is a vision of one heartbeat. This is the One New Man.

One heartbeat means men and women honoring each other, standing together, working together, serving together. One heartbeat means a unified association of believers meeting the needs of those who have been downtrodden by circumstances.

One heartbeat means Gentile believers accepting God's providence and Jewish believers embracing their spiritual children. One heartbeat means Jew and Gentile awakening to the call to walk together as One New Man.

About the Authors

Jonathan Bernis

Jonathan Bernis has worked on the forefront of world evangelism since 1984, taking the Good News of Israel's Messiah to the far reaches of the earth, to the Jewish people, and also to the Nations.

Today, as president of Jewish Voice Ministries International (JVMI), and our associated organizations in Canada and the United Kingdom, Jonathan directs all aspects of the ministry, including the weekly television program "Jewish Voice with Jonathan Bernis," which airs throughout the United States, Canada, Europe, and Asia.

JVMI's mission is twofold: Proclaiming the Gospel to the Jew first, and also to the Nations (see Romans 1:16), and equipping the Church—providing education about the Hebraic Roots of Christianity, the Church's responsibility to Israel and the Jewish people, and how to share Messiah with the Jewish people. The Good News is proclaimed through television, print media, humanitarian/medical outreaches, and large-scale international festivals.

Over 500,000 people have attended our vibrant *Hear O' Israel! Festivals of Jewish Music & Dance* throughout Eastern Europe, India, Africa, and South America. Millions more have participated via television broadcasts. Thousands have responded to altar calls, and about one third of those who have responded have been Jewish. More than a dozen new Messianic Jewish congregations have been birthed in the former Soviet Union through these outreaches. JVMI also partners with several other Messianic ministries to establish and operate Messianic Jewish Bible Institutes around the world to train leaders for Jewish ministry.

The Lost Tribes of the House of Israel are of particular interest to Jonathan and Jewish Voice. A prophetic sign of redemption, as God is revealing these enigmatic peoples from Ethiopia to Eastern India, Jewish Voice has mobilized to reach out with essential humanitarian and medical provision, as God's arm extended in the love of their Messiah. This is a very exciting and rewarding area of ministry, particularly close to Jonathan's heart as these are the poorest Jewish communities on the earth.

A sought-after conference speaker, Jonathan also teaches at seminars and in local congregations worldwide. He is a prominent leader in the Messianic movement and is a passionate supporter of Israel. He has been instrumental in founding many pro-Israel and Israel-Church reconciliation organizations and serves on the boards of several ministries in Israel and around the world. He is the author of several books including, *A Rabbi Looks at the Last Days* and *A Rabbi Looks at Jesus of Nazareth*.

Jonathan is the founding Rabbi of Congregation Shema Yisrael in Rochester, New York, where he served as Senior Messianic Rabbi from 1984 to 1993. He also founded and pastored the Messianic Center of St. Petersburg, Russia, where he lived and ministered from 1993 to 1996.

Jonathan and Elisangela Bernis have two daughters, Liel and Hannah, and reside in Phoenix, Arizona.

Michael L. Brown

Dr. Michael L. Brown is founder and president of ICN Ministries, which is devoted to taking the message of repentance and revival to Israel, the Church, and the Nations. Dr. Brown also served as a leader in the Brownsville Revival from 1996 to 2000. He met the Lord in 1971 as a 16-year-old, heroin-shooting, LSD-using Jewish rock drummer. Since then, he has preached throughout America and around the world, and he is the author of 20 books, including the five-volume series *Answering Jewish Objections to Jesus, Our Hands Are Stained with Blood* (which has been translated into more than a dozen languages), a commentary on the book of Jeremiah, as well as popular books on revival, Jesus revolution, and contemporary moral issues. Widely considered to be the leading Messianic apologist, Dr. Brown is active in Jewish evangelism, debating rabbis on radio, television, and college campuses, as well as teaching the Church about God's eternal purposes for Israel and the Jewish people. He is also a published Old Testament and Semitic scholar, holding a Ph.D. in Near Eastern Languages and Literatures from New York University, and is the host of the nationally syndicated, daily call-in radio broadcast, the Line of Fire.

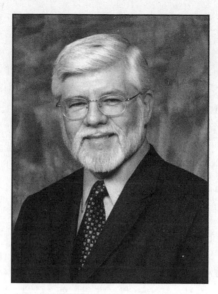

Raymond L. Gannon

Dr. Raymond L. Gannon is the Director of Jewish Voice Messianic Studies Programs with The King's University and has been involved in widespread Jewish evangelism, Messianic synagogue planting, and Bible college and seminary teaching ministries over the past 38 years. After successful Jewish evangelism and discipling ministry in the early 1970s, Ray pioneered his first Messianic congregation in 1973 in Los Angeles. Gannon opened new Jewish outreaches in the San Francisco Bay area from 1975 to 1979, and later pioneered and pastored Messianic congregations in Long Island (1980) and Queens (1983) as well as directing Beth Emanuel Fellowship in Northeast Philadelphia from 1983 to 1988.

Before moving to Jerusalem to co-pastor King of Kings Assembly in 1989, Dr. Gannon taught missions and Jewish studies at Central Bible College, Valley Forge Christian College, and the Christ for the Nations Biblical Institute (New York campus). Upon arrival in Jerusalem, Ray pioneered the Israel College of the Bible, which provided the first successful, on-going, and fully-accredited

Bible college for Israelis. Soon he opened special language departments for Jewish immigrants both Russian and Ethiopian.

In addition to serving as Visiting Professor of Missions and Jewish Studies at AGTS since 1996, Ray has been published in numerous Christian and Messianic periodicals, has authored a column in Enrichment Journal entitled, "The Church and the Chosen People," and is a member of several academic societies. He has held ordination with the Assemblies of God since 1974. In 2003, Ray returned from Israel to assume the post of National Representative for Jewish Ministries with the Assemblies of God.

Dr. Gannon holds graduate degrees from the Assemblies of God Theological Seminary (M.A. in Cross-Cultural Communications and the M.Div.), Princeton Theological Seminary (Th.M. in Church History), California Graduate School of Theology (Ph.D. in Hebrew Bible) and the Hebrew University of Jerusalem (Ph.D. in History). Ray's dissertation topic for the Hebrew University of Jerusalem was "The Shifting Romance with Israel: American Pentecostal Ideology of Zionism and the Jewish State." Gannon was awarded the Hebrew University's highest academic distinction of "Summa Cum Laude" upon graduation.

Mitch Glaser

Dr. Mitch Glaser was born into a nominally Orthodox Jewish home in New York City at a time when views on life, death, and religion were beginning to undergo major changes in American society. His religious roots, fragile at best, were soon lost after his Bar Mitzvah to the excitement and energy of the 1960s. After dropping out of college in 1970, Dr. Glaser moved to California and was introduced to various Eastern religions, which while intriguing him did not answer the questions of his soul. After two of his closest friends received Jesus as Messiah, Dr. Glaser was introduced to the message that Jesus was the Jewish Messiah. Following a thorough investigation of the Old and New Testament along with studying the Messianic prophecies, Dr. Glaser himself received Jesus as his Messiah in November of 1970.

Almost immediately after becoming a believer, Dr. Glaser became involved with what was then the West Coast branch of Chosen People Ministries (formerly known as the American Board of Mission to the Jews). This was the beginning of a 35-year ministry that has included working with such Messianic missions as Jews for Jesus and Ariel Ministries. Since 1997, Dr. Glaser has served as president of Chosen People Ministries—one of the oldest and largest Messianic missions in the United States. Chosen People Ministries was established in 1894 by Hungarian immigrant, Rabbi Leopold Cohn, and today is worldwide with missionaries in nine countries around the world including the United States, Germany, and Israel.

Dr. Glaser has been extensively involved in Jewish evangelism in several countries, and was instrumental in helping to establish a congregation among Russian Jewish immigrants in New York. He is an alumnus of Northeastern Bible College, holds a Master of Divinity degree in Bible from Talbot Theological Seminary and a Ph.D. in Intercultural Studies from Fuller Theological Seminary School of World Mission. He is the co-recipient of *Christianity Today* magazine's Award of Merit in the Apologetics/Evangelism category for 2009, for the book *To The Jew First: The Case for Jewish Evangelism in Scripture and History*, co-edited with Darrell Bock. He is also the co-author of The Fall Feasts of Israel with his wife, Zhava, has written many articles for the Christian periodicals, and has taught at leading evangelical schools such as Fuller Theological Seminary, and Moody Bible Institute. Dr. Glaser is also a musician, composer, and gifted teacher.

Dr. Glaser is married to Zhava Litvac Glaser, a native of Argentina, who has been involved in missionary work for over 30 years. Zhava holds a bachelor of science degree in Judaic Studies from USC (in conjunction with Hebrew Union College), a master of arts degree in Intercultural Studies from Fuller Theological Seminary School of World Mission and a second master's degree in Jewish history. Zhava is also a gifted writer and teacher and serves as both director of communications for Chosen People Ministries and as professor of Hebrew at the Charles L. Feinberg Center for Messianic Jewish Studies. The Glasers have two daughters—Miriam and Jenni.

Jack Hayford

Jack Hayford knows the awesome power of God firsthand. When he was a baby, he was gripped by a life-threatening illness. But as a result of the earnest prayers of friends and family, he was miraculously healed. The doctors had no other explanation except that the grace of God snatched him back from the brink of death. Several years later, Jack was struck down again by sickness. This time it was polio. Church elders anointed him and prayed for his recovery. God heard their petitions and granted a second miracle. These two extraordinary events ignited in Jack's heart a passion for God and convinced him that the Holy Spirit is alive and active in the contemporary church. "Contrary to our preconceptions, God is not economical with healings and miracles. Such wondrous works are frequently attending the proclamation of truth in Jesus' name," asserts Pastor Jack.

Jack Hayford is chancellor of The Kings University (formerly The King's College and Seminary) in Los Angeles, which he founded in 1997. From 2004 to 2009, he also served as president of The International Church of the Foursquare Gospel. He is probably best known, however, as "Pastor Jack," founding pastor of The Church

On the Way in Van Nuys, California, where he served as senior pastor for more than three decades. A prolific and best-selling author, Pastor Hayford has penned more than 52 books and composed 600 hymns and choruses, including the internationally known and widely recorded "Majesty."

He is an acknowledged "bridge-builder," helping to forge healthy bonds among all segments of the Body of Christ. He is recognized for his balance in preaching the Word and avoiding extremes while not diluting or compromising the demands of truth. Pastor Jack's heart to bring unity across all denominational and racial boundaries has given him an open door to minister in all kinds of settings.

Dr. Hayford and his wife, Anna, have four children, eleven grandchildren, and eight great-grandchildren.

Jane Hansen Hoyt

Jane Hansen Hoyt serves as president/CEO of Aglow International, a global network of more than 200,000 women and men from nearly 170 nations who serve 17 million people a year.

Jane has a personal passion to see both genders restored to the strength and purpose of their godly positions for which they were created. As an international leader and mentor, Jane works to empower women and believes they are created with an innate strength and voice to influence the family, church, and community.

Since becoming president, Jane has steered Aglow toward three key mandates: Reconciling the Genders—teaching and training men and women around the world to better understand the strength and authority of God's purposes for each gender; Muslim Outreach—Aglow works to unveil the belief structure of Islam to Christians, while loving the Muslim people by reaching out with news of a God who loves them; Supporting Israel—building relationships and alliances with like-minded groups. Also under her leadership, Aglow has "gone global" through the strategic use of e-mail, social networks, and other mass communications. Today, Aglow can rapidly mobilize more than 1 million women to pray or respond to a crisis.

As a skilled public speaker, Jane addresses conferences around the world, both in Aglow and throughout the broader Christian community. In 2007, Jane moderated a forum on the abuse of women at the first Knesset Christian Allies Caucus Women's Summit held in Jerusalem. In 2009, she was the first female keynote speaker in Promise Keepers' 20-year history.

An ordained minister, Jane has been recognized by other international Christian organizations as a global leader. She serves on the Charismatic Leadership Council, the International Coalition of Apostles, the board of the International Reconciliation Coalition, advisory boards for Christians for Israel, the International Fellowship of Christians and Jews and Morningstar Ministries. She is the author of several books including *Fashioned for Intimacy* and *Journey of a Woman*, and the newly released, *Master Plan*.

Jane is married to Tony Hoyt, former national director of leadership of the Future Farmers of America. The couple resides in Washington State.

Daniel Juster

Dr. Daniel Juster, founder and director of Tikkun International, has been involved in the Messianic Jewish movement since 1972 and currently resides in Jerusalem, Israel where he serves and supports the Messianic movement worldwide. Dr. Juster was the founding president and general secretary of the Union of Messianic Jewish Congregations for nine years, the senior pastor of Beth Messiah Congregation for 22 years, and a co-founder of the Messiah Biblical Institute in several nations. Dr. Juster serves on the board of Toward Jerusalem Council II, participates with Road to Jerusalem, provides oversight to 15 congregations in the USA as well as overseeing emissaries in Israel and the former Soviet Union.

Dr. Juster is an acclaimed international speaker on the relationship of Israel and the Church and an author of several books relating the modern church to the Kingdom of God. His articles have been published in various periodicals such as People of Destiny, Christianity Today, Journal of the Evangelical Theological

Society, Mishkan, and others. He is recognized as a teacher of end-time Bible prophecies and also the meaning of the Kingdom of God and its relationship to Israel and the Church. Dr. Juster, as a Jewish believer in Yeshua, is also an advocate of the Holy Spirit revival in the Jewish community. He has been a speaker at the 1990 Congress on the Kingdom of God, and The National Church Growth Pastors Conference with Dr. David Yongi Cho and Tommy Reid, Larry Tomczak's Covenant Life Church, and also keynote speaker at the national conferences of the Union of Messianic Jewish Congregations and Messianic Jewish Alliance of America, and national Israel Messianic Jewish conferences.

Dr. Juster has taught apologetics since 1971 in various schools. His academic background includes a B.A. in Philosophy of Religion, Wheaton College; M.Div., McCormick Seminary; Philosophy of Religion Graduate Program, Trinity Evangelical Divinity School, and Th.D., New Covenant International Seminary.

Dr. Juster is the author of Growing to Maturity, Jewish Roots, The Dynamics of Spiritual Deception, Jewishness and Jesus, The Biblical World View: An Apologetic, Relational Leadership, The Irrevocable Calling, One People, Many Tribes, and other major works.

Craig S. Keener

Craig S. Keener is especially known for his work as a New Testament scholar on Bible background (commentaries on the New Testament in its early Jewish and Greco-Roman settings). His popular-level IVP Bible Background Commentary: New Testament has sold over half a million copies (if one includes translations and electronic sales). (Naturally, his academic books do not sell so many copies.)

Craig Keener is author of many books, including three commentaries that have won awards in *Christianity Today*. His commentaries include (among others): *A Commentary on the Gospel of Matthew* (Eerdmans, 1999; slightly revised edition, 2009) (also a briefer version with IVP), *The Gospel of John: A Commentary* (2 vols., Hendrickson, 2003), *Revelation* (Zondervan, 2000), *1-2 Corinthians* (Cambridge, 2006), *Romans* (Cascade/Wipf & Stock, 2009).

Other books include (not an exhaustive list): *The Historical Jesus of the Gospels* (Eerdmans, 2009 [available by November]), *Gift & Giver: The Holy Spirit for Today* (Baker, 2001), *Paul,*

Women & Wives (Hendrickson, 1992), *Defending Black Faith* (with Glenn Usry).

Craig's wife Médine, with a Ph.D. from University of Paris 7, currently teaches as an adjunct at Eastern University. Médine was a refugee for eighteen months in her home country in Africa, and together they have worked for ethnic reconciliation in Africa.

Craig has a Ph.D. in New Testament and Christian Origins from Duke University and is professor of New Testament at Asbury Theological Seminary. He has taught in various countries, including pastors in Asia, Africa and Cuba. Craig is also currently one of the associate pastors at an African-American Baptist church in Philadelphia. On rare occasions, he also speaks in other forums (in recent years, for example, for the National Council of Churches Committee on the Uniform Series; for scholarly meetings; and at a diverse range of theological institutions, in recent years including the Assemblies of God Seminary; New Orleans Baptist Theological Seminary; Andrews University; and Wesley Institute, in Sydney, Australia. Asia Pacific Theological Seminary in Baguio, Philippines).

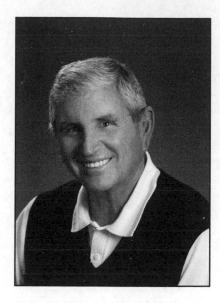

Bill McCartney

Former head football coach of the University of Colorado, Coach Bill McCartney is the founder and chairman of the board of Promise Keepers.

He is also the founder and chairman of The Road to Jerusalem ministry. The organization's mission is to encourage Gentile believers in Jesus Christ to embrace the Messianic Jewish community.

Coach "Mac" led the University of Colorado to a share of the national championship in 1990. He is a member of the Orange Bowl Hall of Fame and the Colorado Sports Hall of Fame, and was honored as Big Eight Conference Coach of the Year in 1985, 1989, and 1990. He won National Coach of the Year honors in 1989.

He is the author of five books, *Ashes to Glory*, *Sold Out*, *Sold Out Two-gether* with Lyndi McCartney, *Blind Spots*, and his most recent, *Two Minute Warning*, co-authored with Aaron Fruh.

Coach "Mac" lives with his wife, Lyndi, in Westminster, Colorado. The McCartneys have four grown children: Mike, Tom, Kristyn, and Marc, and ten grandchildren.

Sandra Teplinsky

Sandra Teplinsky is co-founding director, together with her husband Kerry, of Light of Zion Ministries. From an Orthodox Jewish background, Sandy came to faith in Jesus (Yeshua) at the University of Illinois, where she obtained her B.A. She earned her J.D. from Indiana University School of Law, and obtained seminary training at Talbot Seminary in Los Angeles.

A former litigation attorney, Sandy is now an author and ordained minister. She has been involved with the Messianic movement since 1979. Her passion is to see God's saving and transforming power released on Israel and the Church. Her biblical teaching and pastoral ministry release a prophetic, Messiah-centered, Jewish perspective to God's Word, imparting His love in the power of the Spirit.

Based in Jerusalem, Sandy speaks internationally on God's heart and prophetic plans for Israel and the Church. She also mobilizes intercessory prayer for Israel, both within Israel and in the nations. Her monthly articles, published in international venues, provide in-depth teachings on prayer for Israel. In the 1990s she served in outreach missions to the former Soviet Union, witnessing the unprecedented Russian Jewish revival.

Sandy's books include *Why Care about Israel? How the Jewish Nation is Key to Unleashing God's Blessings in the 21st Century,* published by Chosen Books; *Israel's Anointing: Your Inheritance and End-Times Destiny through Israel,* published by Chosen Books; *The Blessing of Israel*; and *Out of the Darkness: The Untold Story of Jewish Revival in the Former Soviet Union.*

Sandy can be contacted at www.lightofzion.org.

Peter Tsukahira

Peter Tsukahira is a Japanese-American, now an Israeli citizen. The son of an American diplomat, Peter was born in the United States and raised in Japan. Peter became a believer in 1973 and attended Christ for the Nations Institute (Dallas, Texas). He completed a bachelor's degree in economics at Tufts University (Medford, Massachusetts) and enrolled in the American Christian Theological School (Anaheim, California) where he earned a master's of divinity degree.

Peter and his wife, Rita, a Messianic Jew, immigrated to Israel in 1987. Peter is co-founder of *Kehilat HaCarmel* (Carmel Assembly), a Messianic congregation of both Jews and Arabs on Mount Carmel and serves as one of the pastors there. He directs the *Or HaCarmel* Ministry Center and the Mt. Carmel School of Ministry (www.mountcarmelsom.com). Peter travels extensively teaching on the significance of Israel to the kingdom of God and has written two books: *My Father's Business*, about the integration of ministry and the marketplace, and *God's Tsunami*, (www.Gods-Tsunami.com), which explores the convergence of Israel and the nations in God's end-time plan. Peter serves on the board of directors of Church Growth International chaired by Dr. David Yonggi Cho.

Raleigh Washington

Dr. Raleigh Washington serves Promise Keepers both as its president and CEO. He is the founder and Pastor Emeritus of Rock Of Our Salvation Evangelical Free Church in Chicago, Illinois (An urban church reaching across racial barriers in the inner city of Chicago).

He co-authored *Breaking Down Walls: A Model of Reconciliation in an Age of Racial Strife* with Glen Kehrein, the 1994 Gold Medallion winner from the Christian Booksellers Association.

Dr. Washington attained the rank of Lieutenant Colonel in the U.S. Army, earning the Bronze Star for meritorious service in Vietnam. He entered Trinity Evangelical Divinity School in 1980 (now known as Trinity International University), where he earned his Master of Divinity and received numerous awards.

At Trinity, Raleigh developed the Master of Arts in Urban Ministries program, which he directed for six years. He holds honorary doctorates from Trinity International University,

Westminster College, and Azusa Pacific University. Dr. Washington has been a featured speaker for Promise Keepers and many other ministries.

He and his wife Paulette live in Denver and attend Church In The City, a thriving multicultural, inner-city church.

Robert F. Wolff

As President of Majestic Glory Ministries, Robert Wolff speaks insightfully at churches and synagogues as well as on radio and television. He has served in numerous leadership and pastoral positions from Foursquare, to Vineyard, to Assemblies of God across Los Angeles from Lakeview Terrace in the San Fernando Valley at The Dwelling Place, to the west side at Malibu Vineyard and Elements Church in Santa Monica. He contributes his time and talents to organizations promoting reconciliation within the body of believers, including Promise Keepers, Hearts4Zion, and Malkosh (Latter Rain) Ministries. He enjoys orchestrating groundbreaking business, media, and ministry development models at home and overseas. Robert earned a Master of Theology in 1998 from Fuller Theological Seminary in Pasadena, California. He also studied at King's University and Oral Roberts University, both in Van Nuys. He earned his BA degree in economics in 1970 from Colorado College, Colorado Springs. He and his family live in Malibu.

The Star of the One New Man

The Star speaks of the One New Man.
This One New Man is both a person and a people.
The One New Man gains his identity in the person of the Messiah of Israel
and those people who have chosen to follow Him.

The Star represents God's Covenant between
King David of Israel and Yeshua, the promised Messiah.
The boards exemplify the Tree of Sacrifice where Yeshua shed His Blood
for Humanity's Sin as the Passover Lamb.
The interwoven configuration illustrates the Grafting Together of both Jew
and Gentile
as Joint Heirs into the Commonwealth of Israel and the Kingdom of God.

The Six Spikes: Three are Driven In, demonstrating the Finished Work by
our Savior on Calvary.
Three Protruding Spikes point to the Unfinished Work our Lord has called
us to Complete
as One New Man.
It is Time to Awaken to this Call.

Please visit us at: www.awakening1.com

IN THE RIGHT HANDS, THIS BOOK WILL CHANGE LIVES!

Most of the people who need this message will not be looking for this book. To change their lives, you need to put a copy of this book in their hands.

> *But others (seeds) fell into good ground, and brought forth fruit, some a hundred-fold, some sixty-fold, some thirty-fold* (Matthew 13:8).

Our ministry is constantly seeking methods to find the good ground, the people who need this anointed message to change their lives. Will you help us reach these people?

> *Remember this—a farmer who plants only a few seeds will get a small crop. But the one who plants generously will get a generous crop* (2 Corinthians 9:6).

EXTEND THIS MINISTRY BY SOWING 3 BOOKS, 5 BOOKS, 10 BOOKS, OR MORE TODAY, AND BECOME A LIFE CHANGER!

Thank you,

Don Nori Sr., Founder
Destiny Image
Since 1982